The Complete
HORSE

An Entertaining History of Horses

Cheryl Kimball

Voyageur Press

Frontispiece

Cowgirls like Calamity Jane and Annie Oakley may have gotten most of the fame, but women were an integral part of the settling of the West, whether it was in the saddle or behind the scenes at the ranch. (E. W. "Bill" Gollings)

Full title

A mare and her foal is an endearing sight to see. (Photo © Alan & Sandy Carey)

Title inset

The running horse weathervane is common on barns around the country.

Contents

A Paint mare nuzzles her colt. (Photo © Alan & Sandy Carey)

Acknowledgments

A quaint vintage postcard of a woman with her horse.

First published in 2006 by Voyageur Press, an imprint of MBI Publishing Company, Galtier Plaza, Suite 200, 380 Jackson Street, St. Paul, MN 55101-3885 USA

MBI Publishing Company titles are also available at discounts in bulk quantity for industrial or sales-promotional use. For details write to Special Sales Manager at MBI Publishing Company, Galtier Plaza, Suite 200, 380 Jackson Street, St. Paul, MN 55101-3885 USA

ISBN-13: 978-0-7603-2573-5
ISBN-10: 0-7603-2573-1

Editor: Kari Cornell
Designer: Julie Vermeer

Printed in China

Acknowledgments

Many of the photo sources to be thanked are in the photo credits, but of particular note are Gina Gibson and Bill Cooke of the Kentucky Horse Park, Gena McGrath, Rick Larsen, Laura Cotterman, Bob Langrish, Helen Peppe, Piper Ridge Farm, Rick Otto of Ashfall National Park, Debbi Bright, Gwynn Turnbull Weaver, Claire Jett, Freddi Olson, Stephanie Levy, and Sandra Olson for the Botai Settlement photos. Everyone was so prompt and enthusiastic!

I wish to also thank Michael Dregni and especially Kari Cornell of Voyageur Press for their patience and diligence. This book is certainly better than when I sent it in, due to their contributions.

My husband, Jack Savage, acts as "IT department" for me whenever I cry for help. I thank him for that and so much else.

And I would be negligent if I didn't give a nod to my horses. They are a pleasure to have around.

Contents

Never Enough Horses

(or, How Many Horses Is Too Many?)

Show me your horse and
I will tell you who you are.
—Old English saying

A Room with a View
Barn and stall construction varies according to area of the country, climate, and the barn owner's personal preference. Swinging doors, sliding doors, Dutch doors, grille work, swing-out feed tubs, automatic and heated waterers, the choices are almost limitless. But one thing seems certain: Horses, including this Paint horse, appreciate being able to see the world outside their stall. (© Norvia Behling)

Right: Kansas State Fair Stamp
Horse shows and exhibits have always been an important part of agricultural fairs. The very first Kansas State Fair was held in 1878. This advertisement dates from the early 1900s. (From the Collection of Jim Barnard)

Bill, who has been my "grain man" since I bought my first horse almost thirty years ago, has just delivered some hay on a hot, hot June morning. After I write the check, we sit for a few minutes on a bale in the aisle of the barn and chat while we try to cool off a little. The conversation always includes the requisite concern that you can't get anyone to help with hay these days—the kids aren't interested in working that hard, sweating that much, and getting that dirty and tired unless you pay them $20 an hour. And making hay just doesn't bring in the money for that kind of compensation.

"I just know I'm going to love horses all my life. That's why I'm planning to have a career in banking, insurance, and real estate."

Life with Horses

Although there are ways to keep horses relatively inexpensively, this young woman does have the right idea. (*New Yorker* cartoon, May 9, 1988, used courtesy of *The New Yorker*)

Eventually the talk turns to horses. This day, as my five horses lounge in the shade near the barn, we wonder, how many is too many for a person to have? A typical scenario goes like this: You finally buy that little piece of country and get the nice trail horse you've always dreamed of. You worry that Sugar is lonely, so you buy her a pal. Now when you ride Sugar, her pal Red gets lonely. So you get a pal for Red. Now you have three horses. But you can't keep up with riding all three, so a friend or your husband or wife rides with you. But that leaves one of the three

back at the ranch raising a fit when his two friends are gone. So you get a pal for the pal for the pal. And now you have four horses. And once you have four, well, what's one more? And you can't afford to take a vacation because you spend all your money on horses, and you don't have the money to pay someone to take care of them all (plus if you have horses, you most certainly have dogs, cats, and everything else).

Bill's opinion is that you should skip the concern with pals, that three horses is the perfect number—two good riding horses (in case one gets lame) and a young colt to "play around with." I couldn't agree with him more. But I have five horses. Which points to the major flaw with Bill's perfect three: The young colt grows up, adds to your collection of good riding horses, and then you want a new colt to "play around with."

The way to avoid this problem is clear to my husband: Instead of adding to both ends, you sell or give away one of the riding horses when the youngster is added to that group. Then you're back to two riding horses, you get your new play-around colt, and keep the cycle going.

This scenario is perfectly sound except for the fact that my husband—who, by the way, is the first to protest if I announce that I am thinking of selling one of the horses—is into motorcycles. Buying a new one and selling an old one may work easily with motorcycles, but there is a big difference between horses and motorcycles: Motorcycles don't interact with you. Every day you take care of your horses, feeding them at least twice daily, cleaning up, fixing things (sometimes fences, sometimes a horse), and occasionally around all that you fit in a ride. Even more compelling is that the horse has put his complete faith in you—not only to be fed but also to allow you to get on his back, something that goes completely counter to his natural instinct. Not only does he get over that, but he carries you around wherever you choose to have him take you. And for that, he gets sent down the road? Not at my barn.

However, there are times when it is very appropriate to give up a horse. I can do this, it seems, only with horses that belonged to someone else to begin with. I have kept other people's horses at my place for a while and have no problem giving them back. When I lived in Wisconsin, a friend back East bought a filly from my neighbors on no more than a picture and my description. I took care of the filly for the winter and had fun playing around with her, but when I returned to New Hampshire and Carol came to retrieve her horse, I was not bothered by the filly's departure.

But if I buy a horse for myself, I am able to give the horse up only under compelling circumstances. Apparently no cir-

cumstances have been compelling enough these past fourteen years since I've been back into horses; no horse I've bought for myself has left the property yet. I have ninety acres, am self-employed, and have cheap (and many times free) horses being dangled in front of me at the average rate of two per week—I pat myself on the back for having only five!

Bud, Ruby, Cleo, Bugsy, and Willy are my friends. They entertain me. Caring for them, riding them, and working with them relieves stress and carries me through difficult times. That said, I often feel guilty if I'm not riding or paying enough attention to one of my horses. I know I could find great homes for them, but I hear so many stories of horses getting passed from owner to owner to owner that I can't bring myself to let them go.

Did you ever see an unhappy horse? Did you ever see a bird that had the blues? One reason why birds and horses are not unhappy is because they are not trying to impress other birds and horses.
–Dale Carnegie

Ever Curious

Horses are surprisingly curious animals. If you stand at the fence by a pasture with horses, it usually doesn't take long before one of them saunters over to investigate.

Pony Ride

Pony rides are a favored request when nieces and nephews visit Aunt Cheryl and Uncle Jack's farm. Here, twelve-year-old Quarter Horse, Ruby, is providing a little in-the-saddle time for eight-year-old Devon. (Photo by Jack Savage)

I hope *The Complete Horse* will help you understand how this bond between horse and horse caretaker unfolds. Not a day goes by that I don't think about what a privilege it is to be comfortable around horses. And I am apparently not alone. According to a 2004 study by the American Horse Council, the most comprehensive ever done on the horse industry, the industry is alive and well in the United States, contributing almost $40 billion to the U.S. economy.

Although horses are critical to my well being, I was surprised that I had great trouble putting this book together. There is just too much about the horse that I wanted to include. Had I researched every single topic that I thought would be of interest to readers, I would have never finished the book! So while *The Complete Horse* is this book's title, there would need to be several more volumes for the information to be truly complete. These animals have such a rich history and have been too intertwined with humans to be easily summed up.

Instead, I included topics that will entertain readers who don't know much about horses and facts that might surprise readers who do have some horse knowledge. As with any horse book I've written, I myself learned a lot more about horses in the process. I hope it makes you want one in your backyard. Or two. Or maybe five....

Horse as Best Friend

Riding the family horse bareback was a favorite pastime of all farm-raised kids. These horses were typically gentle souls who carried the kids around on all sorts of grand after-school adventures.

World Famous Equestriennes in Daring Feats of Horsemanship

Circuses have been popular since ancient Roman times. In the nineteenth century in America, horses were still main attractions for circus goers. Horses and mules were trained to do amazing feats, like dive from several feet into a pool of water. Circus riders, as this poster proclaims, performed "daring feats of horsemanship."

The Horse Through History

Facing page: Wild Horses on the Run
The thundering hooves of a herd of wild horses has captured the imagination of the human since the two first encountered each other. Typically the herd would not waste energy running without good cause. The message to run would come from the lead mare, who directs the herd's movements, or the herd stallion, in his role as protector. (Photo © Rita Summers)

Right: The Dawn Horse
Little Eohippus, otherwise known as Hyracotherium, arrived on the scene in the American West by 55,000,000 B.C.

Horses are so well studied it has been said that the pathways of history are paved with horse bones. Enough horse fossils have been found that archaeologists have been able to trace the evolutionary changes in the horse down to the subtlest details.

The first known equid, the four-toed *Eohippus*, or "dawn horse," lived about 55 million years ago. *Equus*, which stayed very much the same for almost 20 million years except for slight toe and teeth changes, evolved predominantly in the western part of North America alongside the camel and giant hogs. Imagine how Marlboro ads and John Wayne movies would have looked if the cowboy could have chosen the camel as his preferred mount! If cowboys had been around 55 million years ago, riding camels actually would have made more sense than riding horses, considering that *Eohippus*, which was the size of a small dog, bore little resemblance to the horse that would become a critical tool in the taming of the American West.

The Horse Evolutionary Timeline

55,000,000 B.C. (Eocene Epoch)	40,000,000 B.C. (Upper Eocene Epoch)	30,000,000 B.C. (Miocene Epoch)	10,000,000 B.C. (Upper Miocene Epoch)	3,000,000 B.C. (late Pliocene Epoch)	2,000,000–50,000 B.C. (Pleistocene Epoch)	9000–5000 B.C.	2500 B.C.
Eohippus, the "dawn horse," now known as *Hyracotherium*, is prevalent in the American West, southern England (and perhaps other places). It has three toes behind, four toes in front, and is about a foot tall.	Horses vanish from Europe.	Merychippus, a horse whose teeth, jaw, legs, and hooves were anatomically evolved for grazing in Rocky Mountain high plains, grows to three feet tall. It has three toes all around (precursor Mesohippus had three toes in front, four in back), but the middle toe is becoming more prominent.	Horses vanish from North and South America, migrating over a land bridge to Russia at what is now the Bering Strait. They moved through Asia and evolved further in Europe. Pliohippus has one toe and is four feet tall.	*Equus caballus*, evolved in Eurasia, migrates back to North and South America.	*Equus caballus* becomes one of the most prevalent animal groups in North and South America.	Horse vanishes again from North and South America. The cause has never been determined for certain, but theories range from a plague to being hunted to extinction.	Horse domesticated.

The horse took another evolutionary step 34 to 24 million years ago during the Oligocene era, when it grew in size and evolved to have three toes instead of four. During this era, the horse disappeared from Europe, Asia, and Africa. For the next several million years, the only existing habitat for horses in the world was the western part of North America.

Although changes were already taking place during the Oligocene era, the North American landscape was entirely transformed during the later Miocene era (24 to 5.3 million years ago). Lush vegetation began to disappear, and what was once swampland became a grassy plain. Again, the horse was forced to adapt. Its teeth evolved to be able to chew new sources of food, and its toes developed into hooves to allow it to move with ease through the different landscape. The horse's muscle structure and digestive system changed as well. The horse of this era, called *Mesohippus*, had a brain and molars that were similar to the modern equine.

By 15,000,000 B.C., the horse had evolved to what has been classified as *Merychippus*, the prehistoric horse species that possessed the main characteristics of the modern horse. Still living in western North America, the *Merychippus* was about 10 hands high. It had three toes, but it was starting to develop the more predominant middle toe that would eventually become the single hoof. All that said, you and I could have easily

A.D.1000	1493	1521	1750s	1875	1920	1940	1965—present:
Term "cowboy" used in Ireland.	Columbus brings horse back to South America.	Ponce de Leon lands in Florida with fifty horses.	Horses first shown in North America.	The Kentucky Derby is run for the first time.	Horse population in the United States reaches all-time high at more than 20 million	Mobile tractors take over most of horse's work on farm, prompting many farmers to sell horses to the pet-food market.	The horse population reaches 7 million in the United States, the majority of which are backyard horses.

recognized *Merychippus* as a member of the horse family.

But before the calendar shifted to A.D., one of life's few remaining unsolved mysteries occurred: Horses disappeared from North America for millions of years. No remains of the ancestors of the modern horse, *Equus caballus*, have been found from the early Pleistocene era in North America. Although scientists have never been able to fully explain this disappearance, theories abound. The most accepted theory is that a major catastrophe—a virus, an insect plague, or hoof-and-mouth disease—wiped horses off the continent. By the late Pleistocene era, most large mammals in North and South America are believed to have been killed off by climactic changes and humans who had just reached that part of the world and hunted animals for food.

Eventually the horses returned, migrating back and forth across continental land bridges that linked North America to Asia. Around 25,000 B.C., when it is thought that the earliest migration of Native Americans reached North America, the horse is believed to have been one of the most plentiful animals on the continent.

The horse, ever mysterious, continued to confound paleontologists. Scientific evidence shows that it disappeared from North and South America once again around 9000 B.C., when the land bridge between Siberia and North America vanished and animals were no longer able to migrate via this route.

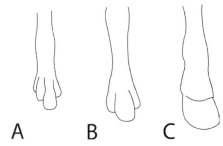

A B C

A Horseshoer's Nightmare

At one time, the horse had as many as five toes to navigate the swampy terrain they roamed early in their evolution. By 10,000,000 B.C., the terrain had changed dramatically and the horse's feet evolved to just one toe, as we know them today.

17

Chincoteague Ponies

A Spanish galleon, off course en route to Peru in the 1500s, became trapped in a storm and wrecked along the eastern shores of what is now Maryland and Virginia. On board the ship were ponies that the Spaniards had brought along to help extract the gold they believed awaited them. When the ship broke up, the ponies were tossed into the ocean. Many of them swam to shore and took up residence on Assateague Island, although that is just one story of how ponies came to live peacefully on the marsh grass and brackish water inlets of Assateague Island for the past three hundred years.

In 1943, the federal government purchased Assateague and split it into two parts: Assateague National Seashore in Maryland and Chincoteague National Wildlife Refuge in Virginia. The pony herds were divided in two, kept separate with a fence, and each herd's population is kept at an average size of 150 animals. The Maryland herd, whose numbers had increased beyond the desired level by 1997, is now controlled by a unique contraceptive administered by dart gun.

Although ponies have been auctioned off since as early as the 1600s, today's popular "pony penning" began in 1924 as a way to control the Virginia herd's population and to raise funds for The Chincoteague Fire Department, which manages the Virginia herd. The ponies that are selected to be auctioned are herded into the waters of the Assateague Channel where they swim to the Chincoteague Island. The first pony to shore is given away to a lucky ticket holder. The rest are auctioned, and those that don't sell swim back to Assateague.

The Chincoteague ponies and the auction were made famous by Marguerite Henry's beloved children's books, *Misty of Chincoteague*, published in 1946, and *Stormy, Misty's Foal*, published in 1965.

Horse Returns to North America

Horses would not return to the Americas until the Spanish conquistadors brought them to the New World in the late fifteenth century. The mares and stallions that escaped from the Spanish herds revolutionized life for Native Americans. Following the lead of the Spanish settlers, Native American tribes began riding horses and collecting herds of their own. The tribes thus became nomadic, following the migrations of the animals they hunted. Tribes began to compete for food and territory, and soon a tribe's wealth was measured in the number of horses in its band.

The Taming of the Horse

As humans interacted with horses, they found other potential uses for these strong animals. And as humans began to make the shift from nomadic hunting to settled farming, they began to shape a different relationship with horses, choosing the more naturally docile individuals to domesticate.

Domestication did not happen all in one place—Western Europe, Northwest Europe, North Eurasia, Central Asia, and Western Asia were all domesticating different types of horses according to the needs of the region. Mountainous Eurasia domesticated stocky small ponies, while Western Asia focused on a small, light, finer-boned horse—what is now known as the Arabian.

Exactly when the horse was domesticated—especially when people first began riding horses—is a little difficult to track. One key piece of evidence has been the teeth of horse skeletal remains; horses that had bits in their mouths showed specific tooth wear. However, just because a skull does not show tooth wear doesn't mean the horse wasn't ridden; it just means the rider did not use a bit made out of a hard material which would be evidenced by tooth wear.

A wooden statue depicting an Egyptian horse and rider hails from 1400 B.C., but Asiatic people were thought to have trained horses hundreds of years before that. Part of the reason that horses may

Assateague Ponies
Wild ponies thrive on Assateague Island National Seashore and nearby Chincoteague. (© Michael Karlin, Shutterstock)

A horse is measured in "hands," a measurement of 4 inches. The Merychippus would have been 10 hands, or around 40 inches tall, much shorter than the modern-day riding horse, which averages 15 and a half hands—written as 15.2.

Westbury Chalk Horse

Several chalk horses dot the British Isles. This one in Westbury was believed to have been cut into the hillside to celebrate the defeat of the Danes in the Battle of Ethandium in A.D. 878. According to the Kennet District website, the original designer was beheaded because the King was angry that the horse was facing away from town instead of toward it. The 182' x 108' figure was redesigned many times, until it was set with concrete in the 1950s. (© Matthew Collingwood, Shutterstock)

Ashfall Fossil Beds Historical Park

The Ashfall Fossil Beds Historical Park, which opened in Nebraska in 1991, provides a firsthand view of fossil-bed excavations. The museum is a joint project of the University of Nebraska State Museum and the Nebraska Game and Parks Commission. Covered dig areas allow exposed fossils to be left as they were found, and special walkways offer visitors full view of archaeologists at work.

Rhinos, camels, horses, and other mammals died here around 12 million years ago, when they suffocated after ingesting ash from a volcanic eruption in the area now known as Idaho. Because of the manner of their death, many of the uncovered skeletons are still positioned the way the animals were when they died. Most have been undisturbed by scavengers, in part because their bodies were covered up quickly with ash. Unique findings at the site include mares with foals tucked in between their legs.

Five species of horse skeletons have been found: the stout, one-toed horse, *Pliohippus pernix*, and the slender, one-toed horse, *Protohippus simus*; as well as three examples of three-toed horses, the stout *Cormohipparion occidentale*, the slender *Neohipparion affine*; the small three-toed horse, *Pseudhipparion gratum*.

Ashfall Skeleton

This is a fully intact (fully articulated) skeleton of the prehistoric horse Cormohipparion occidentale, a three-toed species the size of a white-tailed deer. (Photo by Rick Otto, Ashfall Fossil Beds Historical Park)

The Botai Settlement

In Kazakhstan, an ancient people called the Botai are being investigated in a collaboration by the Carnegie Museum of Natural History, the University of North Kazakhstan, and the North Kazakhstan History Museum. The unique thing about the Botai people, who settled there from 3700 to 3100 B.C., is that their economy was largely dependent on horses. They used horses for everything, including the meat for food, hides for clothing, and bones for tools.

Perhaps most intriguing is the possibility that the Botai may have milked their mares. This finding would make horse domestication a bit older than is commonly thought. After all, the investigators from Britain's University of Exeter and Bristol University pointed out, they wouldn't have milked *wild* horses!

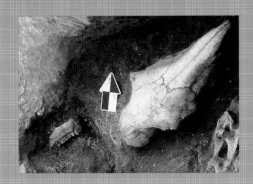

Botai Settlement

The Botai settlement project is just one of many studies that may help further confirm the age of domestication of the horse. (Photos courtesy of Sandra Olsen)

Horses in Mythology

Long before horses roamed the plains of North America, they played an important role in the mythology of ancient societies. The Greeks believed that Poseidon, the god of the sea, gave humans the gift of the horse. Oddly enough, in his entertaining book *The History and Romance of the Horse*, Arthur Vernon writes, "In spite of the fact that his abode seems peculiarly irrelevant to the horse, Poseidon's whole life and interests centered about horses. On one occasion at least, he even became a horse personally."

The legendary white-winged Pegasus was said to have sprung from the earth when the hero Perseus threw down the snake-haired head of Medusa. The goddess Athena gave Pegasus to Bellerophon to train and he took the horse to the Muses to be their private horse. The legendary status of Pegasus meant that gods and mortals alike were constantly coming by to borrow him for one or another of their escapades, including Bellerophon, who rode Pegasus to slay the monster Chimaera.

Pegasus
The horse makes many appearances in the mythological world. The winged horse Pegasus, shown here, is said to have emerged as the snake-haired head of Medusa was tossed to the ground. Pegasus was superlative in every way—white, pure, fast, brave, and highly intelligent.

War Horse
This carving at Stone Mountain, Georgia, memorializes the men and their horses who fought for the Confederacy. Not without controversy, the sculpture was started in 1923 and, with a nearly 40-year hiatus, finally was finished in 1972. (Shutterstock photo)

not have been used for riding earlier was that they were rather diminutive in size compared to today's horses; most were not more than 12 hands (4 feet) tall, making it difficult for them to effectively carry an adult rider.

All in a Day's Work

Long before humans raced horses around a track for the entertainment of an audience, they figured out that the horse could be a very useful work animal. The first horses to serve humans seem to have been draft animals hauling heavy things. Hauling heavy things behind them progressed to hauling heavy things (i.e., humans) on their backs. The horse was ultimately recruited to haul people, cannons, packs, carriages, plows, coffins, and anything else humans could dream up. One key way humans used horses was for riding into battle. In the interest of comfort and safety, and for better strategic riding during battle, stirrups, bits, reins, and saddles were created.

HORSES IN BATTLE

Horses started carrying soldiers and their war accoutrements into battle thousands of years ago. The Hittites invented the chariot in Mesopotamia around 2000 B.C. Horses that were too small to be ridden could pull two or three occupants in the early, heavy, solid-wheeled chariots—at least they could

THE HORSE IS MAN'S NOBLEST COMPANION

JOIN THE CAVALRY
and have a courageous friend
U.S. ARMY RECRUITING OFFICE:

The Cavalry
As this poster shows, the U.S. Cavalry did not underestimate the part that horse played in the lives of their soldiers. (Library of Congress, Prints & Photographs Division, WWI Posters)

over open flat land amenable to crude-wheeled transportation. There were many early chariot models that did not work well and were not even safe to ride in, let alone wage war from. It was the Egyptians who refined the chariot, making it a useful tool on the battlefield and uniting the horse and warfare.

With such advancements in transportation, the Aryans invaded the Persians, the Celts took over Europe, the Hyksos occupied Upper Egypt (for 3,500 years!), and the Hittites spread their empire. Relief artifacts from all parts of Asia often show the heat of battle. Well-muscled horses, trampled men, and skilled archers etched into stone have given a fairly thorough depiction of early battles.

How do you catch a loose horse? Make a noise like a carrot.
–British cavalry joke

The uncovering of Scythian tombs has provided evidence of the extreme to which horses were part of this culture. The brutal but skilled Scythians, who roamed the plains of southern Russia, Siberia, and into Mongolia from 550 to 331 B.C., were among the most noted early horsemen. The Scythians were rich in gold, and had huge herds of cattle and horses. Good thing, since the Scythians considered the horse an appropriate sacrifice during times of war and upon the death of a king. Scythian kings are said to have been buried with their best horses as well as an assortment of concubines and wives. A year after the king's death, Scythians held a giant festival where another fifty horses were slain, skinned, and stuffed along with some of the king's best officers, all as a compliment to the dead king!

From the time the chariot was invented, the horse was a significant factor in almost every war waged in the world until the latter half of the twentieth century. The sixteenth-century invention of firearms and artillery changed the role of the horse in war, but certainly didn't eliminate it. Even today, horses remain a useful military component in some regions.

The statistics of horse casualties in most wars are staggering. In World War I, millions of horses were used and millions died. In World War II, the Russian Army

---

The Hittites are famous for having produced the first manual on horsekeeping and training, which included details on conditioning and feeding and suggestions to improve stamina.

Horsepower

Once domesticated, the horse was used to perform all sorts of tasks, including hauling his own food. (Shutterstock Photo)

The Family Horse

The Amish, who shun modern inventions, still depend on the horse for many tasks. These blue wagons, which carry families to church, to visit neighbors, and to run errands of all sorts, are especially ubiquitous in Amish country. (Shutterstock Photo)

alone used 1.2 million horses in battle, as well as for hauling heavy artillery and supplies. Armies of all countries in the two World Wars scoured their homelands in search of replacement mounts. Even feral horses were rounded up in the American West to supply U.S. troops in World War II.

HORSES IN FARMING

Before the advent of tractors, oxen and horses did the work of the farm. One of the key events in the switch from the use of oxen to horses for pulling and plowing was a minor alteration in the harness. The chest collar designed for oxen cut off the breathing of the horse. After a new harness was made to accommodate the horse, the stronger, faster, more athletic horse took the place of the more plodding oxen.

In some regions, such as the Amish country in Pennsylvania, horses still plow the fields. The Amish are perhaps most well known for their rejection of modern conveniences such as electricity and the automobile. As the world around them began to embrace these new inventions, the Amish found it more and more difficult to buy harnesses and buggies and other horse-drawn equipment; thus they became skilled in making their own. Horses remain a key element in Amish society. In the online version of the *Amish Country News,* many of the contributors' stories

There are small pockets of interested people around the country who continue to use horses for logging work. Horses are considered by some to be more environmentally friendly than heavy logging equipment, especially for selective cutting.

Successful Farming

As illustrated in this charming *Successful Farming* cover from March 1925, the horse played an important role on the farm before the advent of tractors.

SUCCESSFUL FARMING

MARCH 1925

5 cents a copy

Pony Express

The Pony Express is such a legend in the settlement of America that it is a little surprising to realize that the whole enterprise only lasted from April 1860 through October 1861. In that short year and a half, riding for the Pony Express meant you were tough indeed. Horses were changed every ten miles, so the two-thousand-mile route from St. Louis to Sacramento could be run at top speed, a pace necessary to make the trip in ten days. And lest we get too hasty to complain about the cost of today's stamp, the cost to mail via the Pony Express was $5 per ½ ounce when it first started.

The Pony Express was far from a new idea. The Persians had a similar equine mail service a few centuries B.C. Using the same relay approach, the royal mail service covered 1,500 miles in one week.

involve horses. The Amish use horses for everything from plowing to pulling, but the most prominent use is to carry people around in buggies.

CANALS

Huge canal projects, such as the one in eastern Pennsylvania's Lehigh Valley (where the National Canal Museum is located) and the more famous Erie Canal, were undertaken at great expense during the heyday of the Industrial Revolution to move goods, especially coal, which was a crucial energy source in the early 1800s. Canals were a labor-intensive undertaking, both to create and to use.

Cargo was pulled along canals by mules, which walked towpaths lining the sides of the waterways. Heavy cargo such as coal (used for heat as well as for steelmaking) could move easily along the water. The mules worked hard all day long; towpaths were illuminated so the mules could keep cargo moving into the night.

THE AMERICAN COWBOY

Cowboys have come to signify all that is American: the Wild West, vigilante justice, men as tough as nails on the exterior but romantics at heart. As American as the cowboy is, the word *cowboy* was reportedly first used in Ireland.

What Does the Horse Say?

In English, horses say "neigh." Here's what they say in other languages:

Spanish: Relinche

German: Wiehern Sie

Portuguese: Relincho

French: Hennissement

Italian: Nitrito

Polish: Rżenie

Dutch: Hinniken (sounds suspiciously like Heineken…)

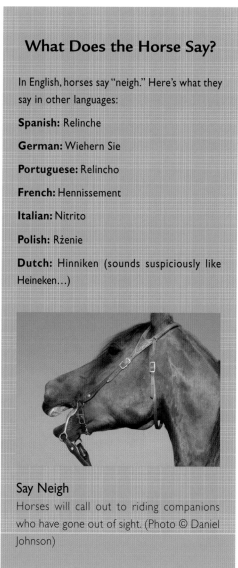

Say Neigh
Horses will call out to riding companions who have gone out of sight. (Photo © Daniel Johnson)

Leggin's

Cowboys use several different leather coverings to protect their legs in the brush and rough country. "Chaps" go from hip to ankle, wrap pretty snugly around the leg, and come in different styles. The leggings shown here, known as "chinks," are open in the back and loose from the knee down. (Shutterstock Photo)

Irish brogue or not, say "cowboy" today to almost anyone and the image that comes to mind is of a weathered man, sporting leather boots and a big hat, sitting astride a sturdy horse, and loping across the American plains alongside of a herd of cattle.

A cowboy (or cowgirl) is defined as simply someone who works cattle on horseback. The American West is still populated by cowboys, but certainly not as many as there were in most of the nineteenth century, during the heyday of western settlement. Tractors, four-wheelers, and even snowmobiles have been employed to do

Bronco Crate Label

Images of the American West were often used in advertising. This colorful, galloping team graced the sides of California orange crates shipped from Redlands, California, in the early 1900s.

Ranch Work

The classic "ranch gelding" is a horse who has been there, done that, has a great work ethic, and knows how to do his job. These horses, when retired from ranch work in their teens, make great backyard trail horses for the casual rider. (Photo by Gwynn Turnbull Weaver)

all manner of farm work, replacing some chores that were once the job of the cowboy and putting a dent in the working cowboy population. As those motorized alternatives to the horse became more accessible, the horse's job on the ranch became more limited as well. One of the inefficiencies of cowboy work via horseback is the time it takes for a young horse to get old enough to use for ranch work—at least two years, and more for more intense work—but most large ranches still pride themselves on having good horse breeding programs. And even today, sometimes the horse remains the best way to reach some backcountry locations.

CITY CARRIAGE HORSES

Where the carriage horse used to be a mainstay on city streets, it is now a romantic

Cowboy Speak

Cowboys have a language all their own. Here's a basic guide to ranch lingo for city slickers. **Buckaroo**: A convoluted version of the Spanish "vaquero," which simply means "cowboy." **Rodear**: A herd of cattle. You might rope a calf out of the rodear to bring it to the branding fire. **Remuda**: A band of horses, usually the group that a ranch's cowboys have at their disposal to complete their work. You might pick a young horse out of the remuda for the morning's long, simple ride to check fences. After lunch you might choose an older gelding from the remuda to spend the afternoon and evening at your neighbor's branding. (The horse doesn't need loads of ground-covering stamina for the branding work but does need to be easily maneuvered in tight quarters and know about working cattle, so the older, more educated horse is perfect for the job.)

Seeing the Sights
Central Park's carriage trade is thriving, bringing visitors to the city through the famous park from morning until night. (Andrei Orlov, Shutterstock)

animals. At least, unlike most horses in the world today, carriage horses have a job. When a carriage horse gets to his stall, he's probably happy to be there!

MULTI-HORSE DRAFT HITCHES

It's been a long time since deliveries were made by the draft horse—the railroad and eighteen-wheelers have taken care of that! But if you can ever catch a multi-horse hitch demonstration at an agricultural fair or other event, I highly recommend watching it. You will be amazed.

In the days when horses were hauling the country's goods around, they needed to back up to the loading dock. Then, while the goods were being unloaded, the horses needed to move out of the way of other passing vehicles. Unhitching them was inefficient so as many as eight large horses, strung out in front of a loaded wagon, needed to shuffle their way to one side until they were standing at a right angle to the wagon. I once watched the huge black Percherons of the Heinz food company's eight-horse hitch perform this feat at the voice and rein commands of the driver. Seeing the horses interact with each other and take subtle cues from the driver to accomplish this feat is a sight to behold.

MOUNTED POLICE

Although the Royal Canadian Mounted Police (Canadian "Mounties") often come to mind when one thinks of horses and

novelty, taking visitors on tours of such places as New York City's Central Park, Chicago's Magnificent Mile, and many other cities large and small around the country. Most carriages travel with traffic. They are well organized for customer use and wait their turn in line like taxis at the airport. Animal-rights activists have attempted to get carriages banned from cities, citing that it is cruel to run the horses on hard pavement and have them work long hours in hot temperatures. The activists have not managed to shut the city horse carriages down, but they have heightened public awareness of how carriage horses are treated, which has likely led to better treatment of these police work, both large and small towns across the United States have embraced mounted police units to patrol their streets. Beach-front communities, such as Hampton Beach in New Hampshire, have a significant influx of summer visitors in a small area and much activity happens right on the shoreline. These communities typically use mounted police to patrol beaches and go amidst the heavy traffic where police vehicles can't easily reach.

Horses in police work receive very specific training. Whereas a pleasure-riding horse would be taught to yield to physical pressure (for instance, if I press my hand on my horse's rear end, she should step away), police horses have to be able to distinguish times when pushing into pressure (such as an unruly crowd) is the appropriate way to behave. And they must remain undaunted by those who might try to scare them.

Police horses play two seemingly opposing roles. On one hand, their size and presence can be extremely intimidating to people unaccustomed to horses, and police can use that fact to their advantage. On the other hand, horses are also very good community ambassadors. Except for those people breaking the law, most love to see the animals on the streets, so mounted officers on patrol can use their horses to break the ice and get to know the residents of their towns. A job as a mounted police officer riding the beach sounds just about perfect to me!

BORDER PATROL

Horseback riders are a natural for border patrol and are employed along international borders all over the world. For instance, horseback border guards patrol the U.S. southwestern border with Mexico and watch for people attempting to cross into the United States without the proper paperwork. U.S. troops in Afghanistan used horses and other equines for border work in that rugged terrain. Horses (and other equids such as donkeys and mules) are simply able to reach places that no other mode of transportation can.

On Patrol

Mounted police are used the world over, from general service in London's busy streets to small towns and busy beaches to special service such as presidential inaugurations. (Shutterstock Photo)

Chapter Two

The Unique Horse

> I can always tell which is the front end of a horse, but beyond that, my art is not above the ordinary.
> — Mark Twain

Facing page: Paint Mare and Colt
A mare grazes among the lush, green grasses of Montana as her colt nips at her mane. (Photo © Alan & Sandy Carey)

Right: San Felice Cigars
A colorful vintage ad from the 1910s declares that gentlemen of good taste prefer San Felice Cigars…and a good horse, of course. (From the Collection of Jim Barnard)

The horse as we know it lives quite a different life from the little Eohippus that browsed and traveled through the swampy landscapes of North America and England. From head to tail, the horse evolved to modern times equipped to graze and roam constantly on firm grassland. In this natural environment, a horse's teeth and hooves would wear down and its sensitive digestive system would remain in balance. But because most present-day horses are domesticated and live in confinement, their owners need to take care of these things for them.

Horse Anatomy

1. mouth; 2. nostril; 3. nose; 4. face; 5. eye; 6. forehead; 7. poll; 8. ear; 9. lower jaw; 10. throatlatch; 11. neck; 12. crest; 13. shoulder bed; 14. shoulder; 15. withers; 16. point of shoulder; 17. breast; 18. arm; 19. elbow; 20. forearm; 21. knees; 22. cannons; 23. fetlocks; 24. pasterns; 25. feather; 26. feet; 27. heart girth; 28. fore flank; 29. underline; 30. hind flank; 31. barrel; 32. back; 33. loin; 34. coupling; 35. hip; 36. croup; 37. tail; 38. buttock; 39. quarters; 40. thigh; 41. stifle; 42. gaskin; 43. hock. (From "How to Select a Sound Horse," U.S. Department of Agriculture)

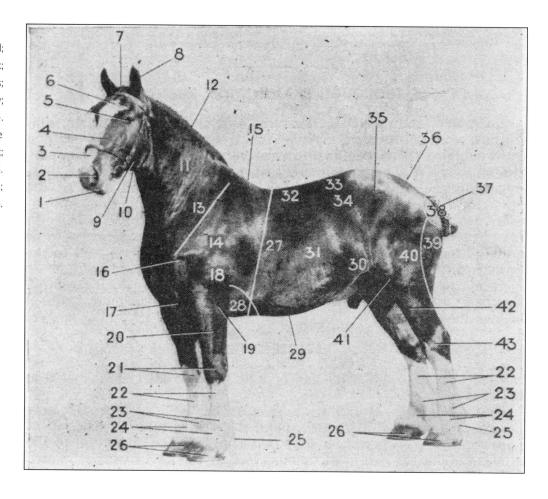

The Horse's Digestive System

Perhaps the most unique feature of the horse is its digestive system. Horse lovers like to say that when digestive systems were being handed out, the horse was hiding behind a door and got whatever was left over. In other words, for such a large animal, the horse's digestive system is perhaps a bit too simple. One of the most common causes of veterinary attention and death in the domestic horse is colic. For horses, the term *colic*, which basically refers to a bellyache, is used to describe any of several digestive upsets, including impaction in the digestive tract and gas buildup. Although horses certainly do get cancer, for the horse owner, colic is the dreaded "C" word.

DOWN THE HATCH

Digestion, of course, begins in the mouth, where the horse uses its strong molars to grind food to a fine consistency. As the horse chews, it shapes the food into a bolus, or ball of food that is of a size and consistency that can be swallowed easily. To aid in digestion, the horse produces as much as ten gallons of saliva per day. The

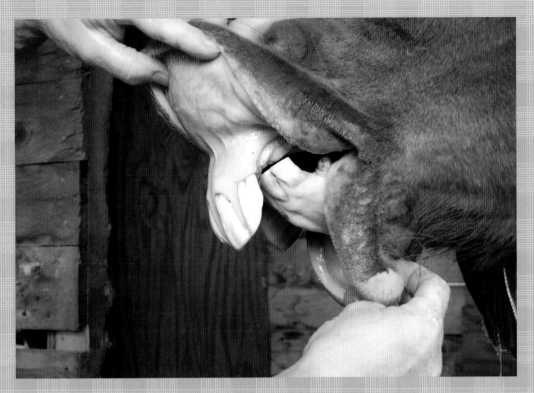

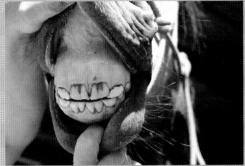

Looking a Gift Horse in the Mouth

The male horse has forty teeth and the female has thirty-six. Two teeth, called the wolf teeth, may or may not be present in both males and females and are not included in the count. (If a horse does have them, they are typically extracted when the horse is young to avoid bitting problems.) It is important that the horse's teeth all wear evenly; uneven wear can cause sharp edges, which can ulcerate the tender skin along the cheek or the tongue and cause discomfort, sometimes enough to make the horse lose its appetite or swallow its food only partially chewed. Poor eating, in turn, can either decrease the amount of nutrition they get out of their food or even cause them to colic.

Grass, the horse's food of choice, is composed of silica, a hard substance that does a great job of keeping horses' teeth well worn. Dry hay and grain do not wear down the teeth as much. If horses are routinely fed these foods, human caretakers need to ensure that their horses get the dental care that nature would otherwise provide. Uneven wear can often be taken care of with a rasp, a procedure known as "floating" the horse's teeth.

Horse owners are advised to have their veterinarian check their horse's teeth at least annually. Some large animal veterinarians have begun specializing in dentistry for horses. They use tranquilizers, power tools, and special equipment such as head rests and mouth speculums designed to help the horse be comfortable (not to mention manageable) during rasping.

Long in the Tooth

This horse's long teeth make him appear to be old, but in fact he has a malocclusion. His top and bottom teeth should rest on each other and stay worn down from grinding against one and other, but because this horse was born with a severe overbite, an equine dentist does the grinding for him. Although fifteen years old here in his domesticated bliss, in the wild he would have been culled in true survival of the fittest fashion. (Photo by Cheryl Kimball)

Teeth Differences

Besides length, another aid in judging the age of a horse is the presence of Galvayne's Groove, a vertical indentation in the tooth which emanates from the gums at around ten years old and recedes over several years. (Photos by Cheryl Kimball)

Horses' teeth are "hypsodont," which means that they continue to grow throughout their lifetime. Thus it is possible to roughly judge the age of a horse by its teeth.

35

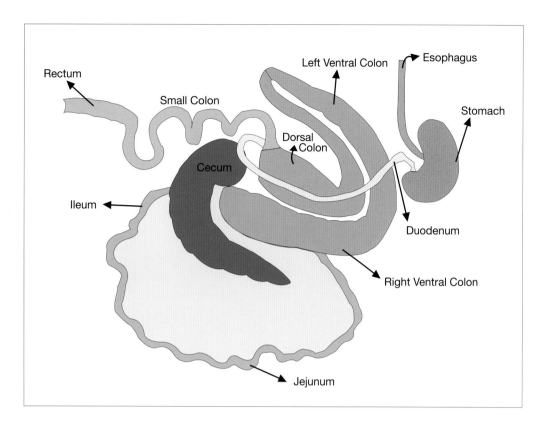

Rectum

Small Colon

Left Ventral Colon

Esophagus

Stomach

Dorsal Colon

Cecum

Ileum

Duodenum

Jejunum

Right Ventral Colon

The Digestive System

The horse's digestive system is perhaps a tad too simple for such a large animal. Because there is only one way out, horses are subject to stomach upsets known in general as colic, a condition that can be life threatening if not resolved relatively quickly.

saliva mixes with the bolus and starts to break down the food. Once swallowed, the food begins the trek down the esophagus and through the upper digestive tract (the stomach and small intestine). A valve, called the cardiac sphincter, leads from the esophagus into the stomach. In the horse, this muscle is so strong that it only allows for one-way passage—once food has gone down it cannot come back up.

THE STOMACH

The horse's stomach holds between eight and seventeen quarts—not much for an animal with an average weight of a half ton. This small stomach is another manifestation of the horse being designed to

eat and roam twenty hours a day, taking catnaps in between. An empty stomach can cause gas buildup and ultimately—here's the C word again—colic.

Unlike a cow, which ingests large amounts of food into the first of four stomachs, called the "rumen," that serves as a fermentation tank, a horse has a single stomach, a system referred to as "mono-gastric." For the horse, then, food needs to be pretty well broken down before it reaches the stomach, where it is merely stored before it moves on to the small intestine. Because most of the horse's nutrient absorption takes place in the small intestine but digestion of fiber and water absorption takes place mainly in the large intestine and the cecum, horses are referred to as "hind-gut fermenters." To run most effectively, the stomach should always be processing food.

For horse owners who want to keep their horses healthy, it's important to realize that these animals were not designed to be fed a huge meal in the morning before they head out to work and a huge meal in the evening when they get home. Thousands of horses have learned to tolerate this schedule—evidence of how much they have been able to accommodate the convenience of their human caretakers. But it is better for the nine-to-five horse owner to find someone to come by midday and feed the horses some hay to help spread out the meals.

Hay Is for Horses

As owner of a five-horse herd, hay is the bane of my existence. Like Goldilocks, who was always looking for the perfect bowl of porridge, I am always looking for the hay season to be just right.

Instead, it is usually too wet. Although wet weather makes the grass grow well, the farmer in New England needs at least three sunny days for dropped hay to cure enough to bale it—more than that if the ground is too wet. If, on the other hand, the season is too dry, the hay simply doesn't grow.

If the hay isn't cut by mid-July, it "goes by" and becomes stemmy and coarse. If the first cutting is done too late in the season, there may not be enough time to get a second cutting in the early fall. Seasoned hay farmers learn how to work around nature, but sometimes nature wins. Which gives horse owners like me migraines wondering where we will get enough hay to last from summer through winter and how much will we have to pay for it. I have learned over the past fourteen years of having horses to be wary of hay farmers whose sole knowledge is based on feeding cows. Cows and horses are polar opposites when it comes to hay. Hay farmers think horses (or horse owners) are just picky, but there are in fact key physiological differences that allow cows to eat poor-quality hay while horses require high-quality, mold-free, must-free, dust-free hay.

The cow is designed to pull in as much feed as it can as fast as it can, then go lie in a comfortable place somewhere and digest. The food heads straight to their largest stomach compartment, the rumen, and begins the digestion process in earnest. When the food is partially digested, the cow coughs it back up again, regurgitating it as a "cud," and chews it some more, before the food makes its way to another stomach compartment and so forth. The key difference is not just that the cow has four stomachs, but the fact that the rumen handles mold, must, dust, and other pollutants before they get to any of the delicate parts of the digestive system.

Not so for the horse. What goes in goes straight through in a process known as "hind-gut digestion." Therefore, what goes in must be pretty good stuff to begin with.

Hay comes in many different flavors, especially from region to region. Trainers often give performance horses at least part of their hay allotment as alfalfa, a high-protein, nutritious legume that sends deep roots into the ground and grows well even in somewhat poor conditions. Grass hays are less nutritious but supply important fiber.

> The fermentation of digesting hay is critical to keeping horses warm in winter. In fact, some believe in feeding horses slightly poorer quality (but still not dusty or moldy) hay in the winter because it is a little harder to digest and therefore produces more heat.

Round or Rectangular?

How hay is baled varies throughout the country. The giant bales shown here both weigh as much as 800 pounds and need heavy equipment to be moved. Smaller 50-pound rectangular bales are the size of choice for many horse owners who don't have a lot of storage space. (Shutterstock Photos)

The All-Important Foot

The outer edge of the hoof is known as the **hoof wall,** the strength of which has a great bearing on the integrity of the whole hoof. The surface of the bottom of the foot (the white area in this freshly trimmed foot) is called the **sole.** The heels have two bulging areas called **bulbs.** The triangular area, called the **frog,** is the shock absorber of the hoof. This horse has just been trimmed, something the horse's hoof does naturally, gradually, and continually when it lives barefoot on differing terrain and is allowed enough area to roam around. (Photo by Cheryl Kimball)

Preparing His Own Food

Before the advent and proliferation of the tractor, horses were not only employed to haul hay, they pulled the machines that cut it, too. (Shutterstock Photo)

THE SMALL INTESTINE

The small intestine is the horse's main digestive organ for protein and soluble fats. It averages seventy feet long and holds as much as forty-eight quarts. The small intestine serves as a major location for nutrient absorption into the bloodstream—as much as 70 percent of the horse's digestion takes place here. Cows, goats, or sheep (all known as "ruminants") have four stomach compartments that break down toxic materials and sort them out before they enter the bloodstream; however, the nutrients in a horse's food go almost directly to the bloodstream before the feed reaches the cecum, a small sac where fermentation occurs and some toxicity can be broken down. Horse owners are often criticized for being picky about hay, but the horse's health relies on it. Food runs through the small intestine in less than an hour, which isn't much time for eliminating toxins.

THE CECUM

After passing through the small intestine, any remaining food takes a side trip through an organ called the cecum. The cecum is around four feet long and can hold as much as ten gallons of food and fluids. The anatomy of the cecum also contributes to colic—there is only one way in and one way out. If the horse does not get enough water, dry feed can block the entrance/exit to the cecum. The further breakdown of feed in the cecum takes around seven hours.

Founder

Next to colic one the most devastating diseases horses face is founder. Founder is sometimes a result of the same conditions that can cause colic, such as getting into the grain bin or overeating on fresh spring grass after a winter of dry hay. Founder starts out as laminitis, an inflammation of the sensitive tissues called "laminae" that connect the hoof wall to the third phalanx, a triangular-shaped bone deep inside the hoof area. When blood flow to the hoof is compromised, these laminae become inflamed and the connection between the laminae and the phalanx is weakened, causing the horse considerable pain.

In advanced cases, the phalanx actually separates from the laminae; without this support, the third phalanx starts to drop toward the ground and can actually break through the bottom of the hoof. Because this advanced condition almost invariably leads to the horse being euthanized, the third phalanx is commonly known as the "coffin bone." It is also why horseshoers are often heard to say, "No foot, no horse."

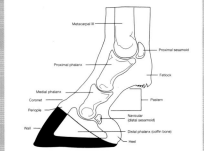

Nail in the Coffin

The coffin bone is held in place in the middle of the sensitive, highly vascular area inside the hoof called the **laminae.** If the laminae is compromised enough through a condition known as laminitis, the coffin bone loses its grip and begins to slant downward, sometimes to the point of coming through the bottom of the hoof. This condition is excruciatingly painful to the horse, is rarely able to be fixed, and typically results in the horse being euthanized.

THE LARGE INTESTINE

The large intestine, also known as the colon, is around twelve feet long and holds about twenty gallons. Here the digestive process slows down; food may remain here as long as two or three days before it combines with water and heads to the small colon to form the fecal balls that we horse owners collect in a wheelbarrow each day.

As an aside, horses produce an average of nine tons of manure each year. I like to brag to all my nonhorse friends as they head to the gym, that with five horses in my barnyard, I tote 45 thousand pounds of manure by wheelbarrow to the manure piles each year. For some reason, they don't seem very impressed.

The Skeletal System

Most mammals have the same general collection of bones, with the odd addition or deletion here and there. (For example, the cow is the only animal with a bone in its heart, and the dog has a bone in its penis.) The horse, however, has some bones that are significantly larger than similar bones in other mammals. For instance, the bones that we often think of as the horse's front knee are actually metacarpal bones, which are the equivalent of the human wrist. The mandible, or jawbone is massive compared to that of humans or small animals.

The horse's foot is exceptionally well designed for the pounding it takes in the course of supporting a half-ton animal. The outside edge of the hoof is known

Directly above the horse's eye is a hollow area in the skull that gives the eyeball somewhere to go in the event of trauma to the eye area. This feature gets more sunken as horses age.

If the Shoe Fits

Although contemporary horseshoers can find themselves working with glue, the good old-fashioned horseshoe nail is still the most common way to attach a shoe to a horse.

For the want of a nail, the shoe was lost; for the want of a shoe the horse was lost; and for the want of a horse the rider was lost, being overtaken and slain by the enemy, all for the want of care about a horseshoe nail.
–Benjamin Franklin

Singular Vision

The field of opthomology has become a strong specialization in the equine medical world. Although horses have fairly well protected eyes—the indentation well above the eye seen here gives the eyeball a place to go to avoid trauma—eye injuries to horses in captivity are common. Many horses have gotten along quite well with just one eye. (Photo by Cheryl Kimball)

as the hoof wall. The flat part, which is white when newly trimmed, is the sole. The triangular-shaped area in the center back of the hoof is the frog, which has an important role in the blood circulation of the lower leg and foot as well as in cushioning the impact of each footfall.

Along each long side of the triangular frog are canals called the bars. Cleaning out the bars of the hoof is an important part of hoof care; if mud and manure are left packed in, bacterial infection known as thrush can result.

The Brain

The horse, which has a brain the size of a walnut, has been accused of being stupid. Why would a thousand-pound animal be startled by something as harmless as a piece of paper blowing in the wind, for example? But a horse's tendency to startle has more to do with its vision than its intelligence. Horses can learn that a blowing piece of paper is nothing to be frightened of, but they need to encounter it; without ever having seen a piece of paper before, they do not innately know that the thing blowing is paper. Would a horse ever be capable of self-reflection or math? No. But as I've often said, people may think horses are stupid but I have never seen a horse smoke a cigarette!

The Lungs

Perhaps not surprisingly, the lungs of the horse are a bit different from most animals. Each of the two lungs are segmented into lobes. Where most animals have several lung lobes (typically two lobes on the right and four on the left), the horse has one lobe for each lung and a small accessory lobe on the right.

These single lobes could be responsible for the horse's remarkable respiratory capacity, something humans regularly witness at horse races. Horses are subject to many respiratory ailments, some just irritating and others more debilitating. This sensitivity is not surprising, given that many of them eat dry, dusty hay and live in dirt paddocks.

Special Features

Like all animals, horses have special protective features. Tufts of hair on the backs of their fetlocks (what we might

Mare and Foals
Early bonding between mare and foal solidifies their relationship. Through smell and sound, each can pick out the other in a crowd. This mare birthed twin foals, a rarity among horses. Twin births in horses do not often reach full term successfully. (Photo © Alan & Sandy Carey)

Just a Few Days Old...

This Paint colt is just a few days old. He will spend around six months with his mom, at which time he will be weaned, a somewhat stressful event for both mare and foal. (Photo by Cheryl Kimball)

In racing and other equine competitive performance sports, horses turn one year older on New Year's Day no matter when they were born. So if a foal is born in May, it could be in the show ring or on the racetrack competing with foals that were born in January. Because young horses grow so fast, an early birth date can be a decisive advantage.

trimmed, depriving them of these natural protections. Because they don't have these hairs, show horses are often kept in stalls where they are protected from bugs and potential traumas.

think of as the ankle area) help direct water that runs down their legs away from their feet. Some horses have longer fetlock hair than others.

Horses have whiskers that work in the same way a cat's whiskers do, allowing them to feel the edges of things. This trait helps horses detect things in the area immediately below their head, which they cannot see with their eyes, as well as in the dark.

Horses also have hair lining the ear pinna (the part of the ear that we can see) and longer hairs at the ear openings. These hairs keep out dust, foreign objects, and insects.

Horses primped for the show ring have whiskers, ear hair, and fetlocks

The Reproduction Slow Lane

Horses are slow to reproduce, typically producing one foal per year. The occasional twins are born and thrive, but most twin births consist either of a single live foal and one stillborn or two prematurely aborted foals. Often, when ultrasounds show twins, a breeder will have one of the twin eggs "pinched off" to better ensure that at least one survives.

The horse's gestation period is eleven months. They are "seasonally polyestrous," meaning the mare comes into heat (is receptive to the male) several months of the year, and there is a period of time—usually early winter to mid-spring—when the mare will not receive a stallion.

The actual birth of a foal is explosive. Where cows may labor over several hours, a mare typically gives birth to a foal within fifteen minutes of the time contractions begin. If it takes longer than a half hour, the horse and foal are likely in big trouble. Although mares usually have their foals without much problem (and notoriously wait until no one is around), when they do have problems it is often devastating for both mare and foal.

In the name of money, humans have intervened in the horse-breeding process to increase production. Many breeding farms turn on simulated natural lighting to bring mares into heat as early in the year as possible. Artificial insemination is common, and frozen semen from stallions is shipped all over the world, allowing even the backyard horse owner in Maine access to the breeding service of a premiere Arabian stallion in Scottsdale, Arizona. The latest technology is embryo transfer, where a high-quality mare is bred to a high-quality stallion and the fertilized egg is transferred to a plain old mare who takes the foal to term leaving the more finely bred mare to conceive again—and again and again—all in one breeding season. This process allows the high-quality mare to produce more than a single foal a year.

Sire of Class

Breeding stallions are the pride of most ranches, large and small. A stallion proves himself in the discipline he is most suited for, winning ribbons, grand champion status in his breed, and various other accolades, which is thought to speak for how his offspring will also fare in competition. Compared even to today's breeding fees, $1500 in 1968 seems like a healthy fee for a breeding, although stallions top in their breed can command much more.

Yum, Yum?

Slaughtering horses for human or pet food is controversial in the United States. Only two states, Illinois and Texas, have horse slaughterhouses. Americans do not eat horsemeat; it is shipped to European countries where people do.

Prime candidates in the current slaughter market are racehorses (both Thoroughbred and Standardbred). Sadly, even some significant racehorses find their way to slaughter, including Racing Hall of Fame member Exceller, who was slaughtered in Sweden after his demand as a stud diminished. Ferdinand, winner of the 1986 Kentucky Derby and 1987 Horse of the Year award, met a similar fate in Japan. These dramatic cases have called attention to the practice of horse slaughter. In a 2005 book, *After the Finish Line*, Bill Heller tells the story of the people working to end racehorse slaughter in the United States.

Other frequently slaughtered horses are a more recent problem, the so-called PMU horses—offspring of mares used to produce Pregnant Mare Urine. The urine is used to make the synthetic hormones used in hormone-replacement therapy (HRT) for menopausal women.

Canada has been home to several large farms where mares are kept pregnant and mostly in stalls, where it is more convenient to collect the urine. The offspring are sold at auction; American buyers from rescue farms go to Canada each year, purchase these foals, and bring them home to either a waiting owner or to find someone to adopt them. Since the negative results of the HRT study back in 2002, these PMU farms have been shutting down, and the mares are being sold off as well as the foals. With this flood in the market, lots of these animals end up at the slaughterhouse.

Horse Burgers

Americans have never acquired a taste for horsemeat. The few horse slaughterhouses that exist in the United States export their meat mostly to Europe, where it finds its way to butchers like this one in Paris. (Photo by Cheryl Kimball)

Chapter Three

Breed Round-Up:
Horses from Around the World

PAIR OF IMPORTED SHETLAND PONIES.

Read any breed association Web site and you will invariably see the phrases "beyond doubt the most versatile of the horse breeds," or "this breed offers a willing people-pleasing temperament," or perhaps "a breed noted for being both bold and kind, can take you where you want to go in any discipline." Everyone loves their chosen breed of horse!

While a horse is a horse is a horse, and they all can be handled with a similar general approach, there do seem to be some key differences among the breeds beyond just the obvious physical ones. Arabians do seem to be a little more fired up and sensitive in temperament, Morgans do tend to like to go, go, go, and the Quarter Horse does seem to have a more laid-back attitude. All that said, when purchasing a horse it is best to consider the individual animal's temperament and attitude, which may or may not fit the description of the breed association's brochure. Coat color, like temperament, can also be breed specific. For example, people often buy Paint horses because of the breed's multicolored patchwork coats.

A canter is the cure for any evil.
— Benjamin Disraeli

Facing Page: An Arabian at the Fence
Fencing for horses is often a personal preference. Electric fencing is perhaps the most common—it is relatively inexpensive, easy to move, and very effective if horses are taught to respect the zap of the electric charge. Vinyl fencing has become popular and simulates the beautiful miles of white fencing that epitomizes Kentucky racehorse farms without the need for painting. Plain wood fencing is fairly safe for horses, but they do like to chew; if wood is used, it needs to be either treated or trimmed with electric to discourage chewing. (Photo © Norvia Behling)

Right: Shetland Ponies
This sketch, titled "Pair of Imported Shetland Ponies," appeared in an 1874 edition of the *American Agriculturist*.

American Quarter Horse

The American Quarter Horse Association is by far the largest breed registry in the United States, making the Quarter Horse truly "America's horse," although the breed has made inroads in other countries as well. (Photo courtesy The Kentucky Horse Park)

While there are many books that describe horse breeds, no general book on horses would be complete without a chapter on the different breeds. There are many, many more than the twenty-eight that are covered here. The selection I offer here covers the general categories of horses (draft, gaited, stock horses, etc.) and includes the most popular/common breeds within those categories as well as a few of the more unusual breeds. By the way, the following breeds are listed alphabetically within general types, not in order of any personal preference on my part. My personal preference would be to have at least one of each breed!

Stock Horses

So-called stock horse breeds are sturdy horses most often used for working with livestock. These breeds are amply represented in the show ring and almost all other disciplines, however.

AMERICAN QUARTER HORSE

While the Thoroughbred is all distance and stamina, the Quarter Horse is the champion sprinter of the horse world. The

top racing American Quarter Horses run their namesake quarter-mile sprint—440 yards—in 21 seconds or less. The Quarter Horse's hindquarters are all muscle and provide the powerful takeoff that makes it good at running short distances and making quick turns. Quarter Horse racing is well established, and purses for the Quarter Horse races are often higher than those in the Thoroughbred-racing world. The Quarter Horse is often the horse of choice for ranch work and working cattle.

The "Celebrated American Quarter Running Horse" was the name early American colonists used for what has become today's Quarter Horse. The American Quarter Horse Association was formed in the 1940s, and the AQHA has come to be the largest breed registry in the United States. The registry comprises racehorses, show horses, and plenty of backyard horses that are kept strictly for recreational purposes. The Quarter Horse is also the favored choice of the cattle ranching industry, which, although having turned some to four-wheelers and other mechanized ways of performing ranch work, still finds lots of use for the good old breed.

Nothing is without controversy, however, and the horse breeding world is no exception. Some people liked the way the Quarter Horse was developing more refinement in its conformation; others

wanted to retain the stockiness of the breed. In 1995, the National Foundation Quarter Horse Association (NFQHA) was created to promote the original aspects of the breed, which some felt had been somewhat diluted by a significant dose of the Thoroughbred breed. The NFQHA looked to promote the so-called "bulldog" Quarter Horse, which is exemplified by powerful hindquarters, a low center of gravity, heavily muscled bodies, good bones and feet, a trainable disposition, cow sense, and high intelligence. Quarter horses registered in the NFQHA must be at least 80 percent Quarter Horse bloodlines, allowing for only 20 percent Thoroughbred lines on the pedigree.

Even the AQHA distinguishes between horses with lots of Thoroughbred bloodlines. Known as "appendix" Quarter Horses, any horse that is a cross between a registered Quarter Horse and a registered Thoroughbred, or that is the offspring of a Quarter Horse–Thoroughbred cross and a pure Quarter Horse, has an *X* in front of its registration number, indicating it is not registered in the main QH registry, but in the registry's appendix.

The Quarter Horse tends to live up to its reputation as a reliable, even-tempered, strong, and comfortable horse. Although there are always exceptions to any stereotype, Quarter Horses are prized for being steady mounts with a low "flappability" factor. Once well exposed to life, nothing

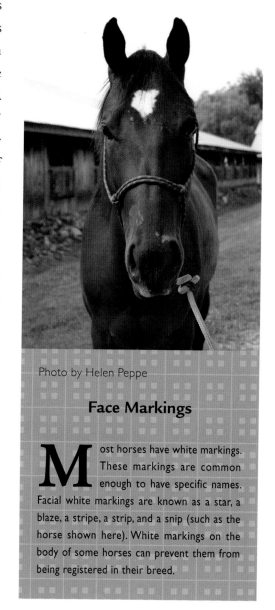

Photo by Helen Peppe

Face Markings

Most horses have white markings. These markings are common enough to have specific names. Facial white markings are known as a star, a blaze, a stripe, a strip, and a snip (such as the horse shown here). White markings on the body of some horses can prevent them from being registered in their breed.

Appaloosa

The colorful Appaloosa's name is a derivative of the agriculturally fertile Palouse region of southeastern Washington and northwestern Idaho. (Photo © Alan & Sandy Carey)

much fazes them. And for ranch work, they have the added advantage of being sturdy enough to start under saddle at younger ages (typically two).

APPALOOSA

The Appaloosa was named by white settlers for the Palouse region of eastern Washington state, where the Nez Perce Indians developed the splashy-coated breed. The classic Appaloosa has a "blanket coat," consisting of a more uniform color along the front of its body and a blanket of spots splashed across its rump. However, the "leopard" Appaloosa, which has spots all over its body, is also quite fashionable. Other characteristics of Appaloosas are mottled skin around the muzzle, eyes, and gentalia and white–and–black striped hooves. Tails and manes are typically wispy, a trait encouraged as it prevents tangling with brush and burrs.

The Appaloosa is a sturdy breed that the Nez Perce selectively developed for intelligence and speed. The Appaloosa Horse Club was founded in 1938 to protect the breed after decades of decline following the Nez Perce defeat in the late 1800s.

Appaloosas were selectively bred for stock use, but today they are found in every aspect of the horse world, from showing and jumping to racing and endurance distance riding. They tend to be compact and of average height, ranging from 14.2 to 15.2 hands.

PAINT

The Paint horse is a breed of stock horse whose characteristics include very specific color patterns. These patterns must combine white and one or more of the classic horse colorings such as chestnut, bay, brown, or black.

That isn't where the breed requirements end, however; the Paint horse must also be of the classic stock horse type,

Paint Horse
The Paint horse is known as a "color breed," with color patterns being a key breed characteristic. Some purebred Paints have no markings; they are referred to as "breeding stock Paints"—if bred to another purebred Paint, this individual could well produce a colored foal. (Photo by Bob Langrish)

having well-muscled hindquarters and strong bones.

How did the Paint horse become such a classic American horse? The early Spanish explorers brought two-toned horses to North America with them; Hernando Cortez specifically brought one sorrel-and-white horse to the New World in the early sixteenth century. Some of these horses escaped to freedom and joined existing wild horse herds or created their own.

While many depictions of Native Americans show a brave warrior astride a loudly colored Paint horse, the American cowboy loved Paints as well. (Baby boomers will remember Little Joe and his Paint horse from the popular television show *Bonanza*.)

People often confuse Paint horses and Pintos. The word "Pinto" is directly derived from the Spanish word *pintado*, which means "painted." The Pinto can be almost any breed; its classification as a Pinto is determined by its colorful coat. The Paint horse, however, is a specific breed with registration requirements that go well beyond color. To be registered with the American Paint Horse Association, a Paint horse's sire or dam must be registered with the American Paint Horse Association, the Thoroughbred Jockey Club, or the American Quarter Horse Association.

Hot-blooded Horses

"Hot-blooded" is the term used to refer to the horse breeds that originated in the

Saddlebred

The tall, elegant Saddlebred was a favorite among American war generals such as Lee, Grant, and Jackson. (Photo by Helen Peppe)

warmer regions of the world (although members of this category don't necessarily have their roots in the desert). They tend to have thinner skin, which allows for faster cooling. Because they developed in areas of poor grazing and had to seek food in wide-open terrain, they evolved to be extremely fleet of foot to escape predators.

AMERICAN SADDLEBRED

With a lineage that can be traced back to Paul Revere's Naragansett Pacer mount on his famous ride, "The American Horse," as the Saddlebred was once known, has been witness to a significant amount of America's colonial history. From the Revolutionary War to Daniel Boone's trek through the Cumberland Gap into Kentucky, to the War of 1812, Saddlebreds were the mount of choice. But the real advance of the breed came during the Civil War, when Generals Lee, Grant, Sherman, and Jackson rode Saddlebreds Traveller, Cincinnati, Lexington, and Little Sorrell respectively.

The Saddlebred's registry was established in 1891 and was the first breed association established in the United States. Although today this elegant breed is mainly a show horse, the Saddlebred is very versatile and had its beginnings as a "using horse"—one that had a job to do. Standing tall, at an average of 16 hands, with a slender body frame, the Saddlebred cuts an impressive figure.

This breed of horse has a naturally high step to its gait. The show world, which often adheres to the classic adage "if some is good, more is better," fits these horses with artificially tall and heavy shoes to accentuate that action. If allowed to have more natural trimming and shoeing, the Saddlebred is quite capable of performing cow work, jumping, or trail riding.

ANDALUSIAN

Think of the impressive horse ridden in the Portuguese bullfighting ring, and you would be thinking of the Andalusian. This horse of the Iberian Peninsula has

Andalusian
It is easy to see why a matador might choose the impressive Andalusian for his mount in the bull ring. (Photo courtesy The Kentucky Horse Park)

Arabian

Thought by many to be the most versatile breed of all, the Arabian has had a huge influence on almost every breed of horse. (Photo by Helen Peppe)

many variations, including the Luisitano and the Carthusian, although all are basically the same horse with minor differences in characteristics. The Andalusian originated in the Middle Ages when the Moors, who invaded Spain in the seventh century, bred their Barb horses with the native Spanish stock.

Especially in Europe but also in the Americas, only the Arabian has been more influential on other breeds of horses than the Andalusian. The Andalusian is the foundation for the Lipizzaner breed, the white horse familiar to many from its long association with the famed Spanish Riding School of Vienna and the spectacular shows the school performs around the world.

The Andalusian is typically grey (a color most people would say is white) and stands at an average height of 15.2 hands. The horse sports a flashy mane and tail and a massive arched neck. The breed, considered to be intelligent and kind, was at one time bred and trained by monks in Spain. When Napolean invaded Spain and stole horses, monks hid an Andalusian herd and eventually the breed was re-populated.

ARABIAN

Almost all purebred horses can eventually trace their breeding back to the Arabian. Most breeds recognized today have had significant influence from the Arabian breed; however, three specific breeds—the Morgan, the Standardbred, and the Thoroughbred—can all trace their lineages to three Arabian stallions: the Byerly Turk, the Darley Arabian, and the Godolphin Arabian.

Throughout history, Arabians have been bred with great care. It is said that the Bedouins, the Middle Eastern tribe that originally bred the horses, brought their mares and foals into the family tent to live. Legend has it that the Arabian's history stretches as far back as 3,000 B.C. In around A.D. 780, an Arab historian, El Kelbi, researched and wrote about the history of the breed. King Solomon's royal stables were said to have held hundreds of Arabian saddle horses and thousands of chariot horses.

Germany, Hungary, Poland, Russia, and France all bred Arabian horses in the eighteenth and nineteenth centuries. But it was the Crabbet Stud of England that was the foundation for the breed's development in the United States.

Arabians possess great endurance, stamina, speed, courage, and versatility. To top it all off, they are especially beautiful horses with an amiable temperament. Arabians are prized for their arched necks, high tail carriage, and petite faces that have an indentation at the lower bridge of the nose referred to as "dished." Anatomically, the Arabian is unique in that it has one less rib and one less vertebra than other horse breeds. They range in height from 14.2 to

15.2 hands, but tend toward the shorter side. Arabians excel in many activities, but are used extensively for endurance long-distance trail riding. There is also a very active Arabian racing contingent.

MORGAN

Although not your classic hot-blooded horse, the feisty little Morgan perhaps belongs in this category more than any other breed. Here is a breed with a story to tell. Although shopworn, the tale says that a compact two-year-old colt by the name of Figure was given to Vermont schoolteacher Justin Morgan in 1791 as payment for a debt. The horse was a fine looking animal with great qualities, but he was small, so no one was interested in buying him. Justin Morgan began to use the horse himself. He pitted Figure against all breeds, types, and sizes of horses in races and pulls. Figure never gave up and almost always came out the winner. The little horse became known around Vermont as "Morgan's horse." Figure was a sound horse that lived for

Morgan

Like many breeds, the Morgan has branched off into a more refined Saddlebred-style horse and the classic stocky horse of the breed's original form. (Photo © Bob Langrish)

Morgan
When shown "at halter," opposed to "under saddle," horses are taught to stretch out and show off their physical traits. (Photo © Bob Langrish)

thirty years, working hard almost every day of his life. His gentleness with children, fast-moving gaits, and spirit made him a desirable breeding horse, and he sired many offspring, including three great Morgan foundation stallions: Bulrush, Woodbury, and Sherman.

Morgan horses made their way to the cavalries and the battlegrounds of the Civil War, and today there is a distinction between refined "show Morgans" and stocky government remount lines, the horses that replaced killed or wounded horses from the battleground. The

Morgan was also instrumental in building the American countryside, clearing woods and mountainsides, and bringing the colonists to town in smart carriages. Morgans also made their way west, helping their owners answer to the call of gold in California.

Today's Morgan stands between 14.2 and 15.2 hands, but many individual horses lean toward the smaller height of their famous ancestor. They tend to be brown, bay, or chestnut in color and are often used in therapeutic riding schools and by mounted police. The Morgan has greatly influenced the Saddlebred, Standardbred, and Tennessee Walking Horse breeds.

STANDARDBRED

The Standardbred is second only to the Thoroughbred in racehorse value. While Thoroughbred racing is "under saddle" meaning the jockey rides on a saddle atop the horse, Standardbreds are raced "under harness"; a harness connects the horse to a two-wheeled cart known as a sulky, where the jockey rides. The name "Standardbred" was first used in 1879; the term referred to an individual horse that met a racing standard (a mile in 2.30 minutes or less) in order to be included in the Standardbred registry. The Standardbred traces its lineage back to an English Thoroughbred named Messenger who was ultimately exported to the United States. Every Standardbred can trace its heritage back to Hambletonian, a great-grandson of Messenger. Hambletonian's offspring went on to overtake the Morgan as the fastest harness-racing horse.

Standardbred
These two Standardbred foals spend their time growing strong and healthy in preparation for a life on the racetrack. (Photo by Helen Peppe)

Thoroughbred

Most people, knowledgeable about horses or not, know the powerful Thoroughbred horses of racetrack fame. (Photo © Bob Langrish)

The word "thoroughbred" is often confused with "purebred." A purebred horse is a member of a specific breed whose dam and sire were both also purebred members of the breed. Thoroughbred is itself a breed of horses, and those horses whose dams and sires are both Thoroughbred are purebred Thoroughbreds.

In conformation, the Standardbred is a sturdier horse than the more sleek and refined Thoroughbred. The legs are strong, and the hooves are extremely sound. The most valuable Standardbreds in the United States are raised on the same Kentucky bluegrass as their more famous racing counterparts.

The Standardbred moves differently from the Thoroughbred as well. The Standardbred's gait for racing is a lateral trot called "pacing," where both legs on the same side move at the same time, opposed to the "diagonal" trot of the Thoroughbred (and most horses) where the opposite front/hind leg move forward simultaneously.

Standardbreds range from 14.1 to 17 hands. They are usually bay, brown, or chestnut in color, but can occasionally be other colors as well. Retired racing Standardbreds (which range in age from two years old to teenaged) are used for pleasure riding and driving.

THOROUGHBRED

Most people, horse lovers or not, will recognize the powerful Thoroughbred horse pounding around the racetrack, carrying jockeys on paper-thin saddles, their brightly colored silks flapping in the wind.

The Thoroughbred horse was developed in England in the eighteen and nineteen hundreds for the sport of racing. For a breed so young, the Thoroughbred has had a significant influence on the entire modern horse world.

The Jockey Club is the registering association for all Thoroughbreds in North America. The club was formed in New York City in February 1894 by a group of breeders and owners who were looking to organize what had become a chaotic sport. The Jockey Club continues to have an office in New York as well as in Lexington, Kentucky, the racehorse capital of the world.

The club keeps all records of registered Thoroughbreds in its famous American

Stud Book, which dates back to 1896. Roughly thirty-six thousand racehorses are registered each year. Stables can also register their name and silk colors with The Jockey Club, although stables are only *required* to register with The Jockey Club if they are racing a horse on a New York State racetrack.

Unlike other breeds, which are sometimes bred through artificial insemination and embryo transfer, Thoroughbreds are required to be bred only by "live cover." In other words, the mare and stallion must both be in the room.

Warmblood Horses

"Warmblood" is a collective term for a group of European-based breeds whose body type, temperament, and carriage place them between the cold-blooded draft horses and the hot-blooded horses such as Thoroughbreds and Arabians. They are large saddle horses, standing an average of 17 hands tall.

Unlike other breed families, the Warmblood breeds are required to go through a rigorous pedigree documentation and performance-ability tests in order to enter a Warmblood breed registry. Each Warmblood breed has different testing requirements, but tests almost always include actual performance testing, such as the three-phase events of dressage, jumping, and cross country.

Dutch Warmblood
The tall Warmblood breeds—Dutch, Swedish, Holsteiner, Hanoverian, and others—have become popular mounts for dressage and event riders. (Photo by Helen Peppe)

DUTCH WARMBLOOD

The Dutch Warmblood was developed from two native Dutch breeds—the Gelderlander and the Groningen (which were greatly influenced by the Freisian, another Dutch breed). Dutch Warmbloods were originally bred to be sport horses for use in competitive recreational events, such as jumping, dressage, and competitive driving. Prior to World War II, however, the breed was used extensively in farming. After the war and once machines began to displace the horse in farm work, the breed once again became a sport horse. Other Warmblood breeds and Thoroughbreds were used to influence the revitalized competitive Dutch Warmblood.

Hanoverian

The Hanoverian is a relative newcomer to the United States, with a breed registry opening in 1978. (Photo by Helen Peppe)

In 1535 and 1541, during the reign of Henry VII, acts were passed that made it illegal in Britain to breed any horse that stood under 15 hands. Exportation was also prohibited. Strong horses were the flavor of the day, because of their extensive use in battle.

HANOVERIAN

Among the Warmbloods, the Hanoverian represents everything that is best about the Warmblood horse. The breed originated in an area of northern Germany where horses have been bred intensely for more than four hundred years.

Hanoverians are well proportioned, calm under pressure, and have a very natural, smooth, elastic movement. They are known to be willing and giving partners and have become one of the more prominent saddle horses found on all continents. The American Hanoverian Society was established in 1978 to promote and monitor the breed in the United States.

HOLSTEINER

Before farming became mechanized, the Holsteiner was a critical part of the German farmer's livelihood. The breed was also used as military stock, carriage horses, and just plain saddle horses. The Holsteiner had a significant influence on other European Warmblood breeds.

The Holsteiner was named after the northernmost province in Germany where the breed developed. After World War II, when the need for horses in the military and in farming began to decline, the Holsteiner was bred with Thoroughbred lines, which helped to not only refine the breed and soften some of its coarser physical characteristics, but also to refine the Holsteiner's movement as well. Today, the typical Holsteiner has finer facial features and a smoother gallop than its predecessors; it is also faster. It has become the performance horse of choice for riders competing in jumping events and three-phase competitions. The Holsteiner can run a cross-country course with impressive breadth and speed, but it is also able to perform elegantly in the dressage ring. The main breeding association for the Holsteiner remains in Germany where it originated.

Draft Horses

Before the advent of tractors, there were the workhorses. These massive equine specimens were the lifeblood of any farm, and they were used to transport goods from freight yards through city streets to customers as well. But once the tractor took hold and farmers gave up their horses for machinery, draft horses became much less prominent.

Today the various draft horse breeds are novelties, bred by those who simply love draft breeds and use them for hayrides, sleigh rides, and pulling contests at the county fair. Several companies have draft-team mascots—Anheuser-Busch has its famous Clydesdales, Heinz has a Percheron eight-horse hitch, and Harrods has a Friesian team.

BELGIAN

The Belgian horse takes its name from its homeland, an agricultural mecca where farmers needed a heavy breed of horse to help with pasture mowing and haying. As with all draft breeds, Belgians take some of their ancestry from Julius Caesar's Great Horses, known for use in battle throughout the Roman Empire.

American interest in this breed came about after the Belgians exhibited their draft breed at the St. Louis World's Fair in 1903. Importation picked up considerably and lasted until 1914 when World War I halted all importation. Breeders in the United States began to use their existing stock to develop the Belgian breed.

The most significant period in the Belgian's history in the United States was between 1981 and 1985, when a record number of the breed were registered or transferred. The breed continues to be popular; the U.S registry is maintained in

Wabash, Indiana, where it was founded in the late 1880s.

The American version of the Belgian horse is almost exclusively chestnut in body color, with four white socks and a flaxen mane and tail.

Holsteiner
The main breed association for the Holsteiner remains in the province of Germany where the breed was developed. (Photo by Cheryl Kimball)

Belgian
Belgian draft horses are often used for hauling wagons, pulling plows, and logging. (Photo by Laura Cotterman)

59

CLYDESDALE

The Clydesdale originated in the Clyde Valley in Scotland. The saying "no foot, no horse" was taken seriously with the Clydesdale, which is known for straight legs and sturdy feet. The development of large, flat feet made it a good breed for hauling loads along city streets, but less suited for field work since its feet were often too large to fit in the furrows. Just as the Shire was key to the development of the United States, the Clydesdale went to work building Australia.

Never as large as the Shire, the Clydesdale of today is even less substantial than it was during the breed's early years. Clydesdales average 16.2 to 18 hands and typically weigh less than a ton, but there are always individual exceptions. The Clydesdale is commonly bay in color, but other colors, including roan, are acceptable as well. Classic markings

Facing page: Belgian Mare and Foal
Most foals start life pretty timid and stick close to mom, a smart instinct in a prey animal such as the horse. As a foal gains confidence, it will venture farther and farther from its dam, often spending considerable time with other foals in the pasture. Mares can be quite protective; a breeder is often cautious about how a first-time mother will react to humans handling her newborn foal. (Photo © Alan & Sandy Carey)

Above: Clydesdale
Anheuser-Busch made the Clydesdales famous with their "Budweiser Clydesdales," commonly seen in Super Bowl beer commercials. (Photo © Bob Langrish)

Friesian

The Friesian is a striking draft breed—always pitch black with flowing manes, sometimes the manes are so long they drape on the ground. (Photo courtesy The Kentucky Horse Park)

are four white socks up to the knee and hock length.

FRIESIAN

This stunning black draft horse of the Netherlands is the distinct ancestor of the Shire horse and has had significant influence on other draft breeds as well. The Friesian breed was enhanced by a cross with Andalusians during the Eighty Years War, when Spain occupied the Netherlands from 1568 through 1648.

In 1913 there were only three Friesian stallions left in the world. The breed was brought to the brink of extinction for several reasons, including a predominance of crossbreeds that overtook the Friesian's influence in the trotting races. But World War II brought fuel and vehicle shortages, and the Dutch returned to their draft horses to supply the power they needed to run their farms.

Friesians are always pitch black with flowing manes and tails that often reach the ground. At one time, Friesians tended to be small for draft horses, averaging around 15 hands, although modern breeders are creating taller horses. Friesians have found their way to the dressage world and are often crossed with Thoroughbreds to increase their skill in competition.

PERCHERON

This impressive draft breed is typically black or grey. The Percheron originated somewhere in the Le Perche region of France as a carriage horse. Mares of native Le Perche stock were bred with Arabian stallions during the eighth century to create the breed we know today.

Percherons

Percherons are an enormous, powerful draft horse breed originally from the Le Perche region of France. They were imported to the United States in 1839. (Photo © Bob Langrish)

Standing only 15 to 16 hands tall, the early Percherons were smaller than the classic draft horse, but their size made them more versatile. When other horses began to take over the Percheron's carriage duties, breeders abandoned plans to breed smaller horses, and the Percheron became a larger, more capable workhorse. By the nineteenth century, Percherons joined the ranks of army remount horses. During that same time, a horse named Jean LeBlanc was born; all modern Percherons can trace their lineage back to this stallion.

In 1839, Edward Harris of Moorestown, New Jersey, imported two Percheron stallions to the United States. The Dunham family of Ohio bought one of the two stallions and formed a breed association for Percherons.

Teamsters used Percherons extensively to move goods. During the 1930s and 1940s, Percherons roamed city streets delivering freight. But like many horse breeds, the Percheron saw a decline at the end of World War II, when many tasks that were once performed by horses were taken over by machines. The cottage farmer and forester keep the breed alive today, using the horses in recreational activities such as hayrides and parades.

SHIRE

Another grand member of the draft horse breeds is the Shire horse, a breed that has come to be known for its strength, energy, and endurance.

Shires are descended from Julius Caesar's Great Horses, a collection of

Studbooks

Studbooks contain the pedigree documentation of the various breeds. Many studbooks are "closed," meaning membership is open only to those animals with parents already in the studbook. An 'open' studbook allows for more crossbreeding by allowing any breed of horse to become a member. The only requirement is that the horse's sire and dam must be registered in a studbook for their own breeds. Open studbooks are typical of most of the Warmblood breeds, which are by definition crossbred horses, usually with lots of Thoroughbred influence.

The Shire breed association began in Britain in 1876 as the English Cart Horse Society and changed its name to the Shire Horse Society in 1884. Like all draft breeds, the Shire lost ground after World War II and perhaps owes much of its current revival in England to the breweries that continue to use horses to represent their industry.

Physical characteristics of the Shire include a massive arched neck, shoulders particularly suited for the collar, considerable feathering on the fetlocks, and well-muscled legs. Its coat color is often black, but can be other standard horse coat colors such as bay and grey. The Shire horse typically weighs in at more than a ton and stands 19 hands tall.

Shire
The Shire may well be the largest of the horse breeds, commonly standing at 19 hands and weighing more than a ton. They originated in Britain, where their association was known as The English Cart Horse Society. With the most common use of the modern horse being riding or racing, the massive Shire horse doesn't fit in well with either of these uses. (Shutterstock Photo)

animals he prized for their exemplary service as war horses; these Great Horses were well suited to carry the considerable weight of an armor-clad rider. The English were enamored with the breed and used their well-developed expertise in breeding and making pedigree improvements to develop exactly the horse they needed to carry heavy loads over rough streets. In the early United States, Shire was the breed of choice for moving goods in a developing young nation. The horses were a popular U.S. import before World War I.

Gaited Horses

Gaited horses are breeds that are genetically predisposed to be trained to perform gaits other than the standard walk, trot, and canter. The gaited horse breeds are used when riders need to cover ground comfortably and efficiently. Riders with back problems, who require a horse with a smooth, even stride, often favor gaited horses.

ICELANDIC

Aficionados of the diminutive Icelandic breed will quickly correct you if you try to call these horses "ponies." Even though it is pony sized, the Icelandic is not considered a pony breed; Icelandics are gaited horses. They are prized animals in their native land, where the horses are extremely healthy, and their disease-free status is fiercely protected. A horse that is exported from Iceland is never allowed to return. Even used horse tack is not allowed into Iceland.

Settlers brought horses to Iceland more than eleven centuries ago, and the Icelandic is a descendent of these imports. Its first breed association was formed in 1904.

These sturdy little horses have quite the precocious personality, but are strong and hard working. They are sure footed, able to carry sizeable adults long distances, and easy to feed and house. Icelandics are commonly chestnut in color, but every color, with the exception of Appaloosa markings, is acceptable.

The Icelandic has a unique gait called the "tolt," which is described as a "running walk." Some Icelandics are able to

Icelandic

Icelandic Horses may be diminutive in physical size, but they are strong, sturdy mounts that can comfortably carry a grown adult. Iceland is very protective of their horses—exported individuals are never allowed to return to their homeland and the country does not even allow used tack to be brought into the country. (Photo © Bob Langrish)

Paso Fino

The Paso Fino is one of many gaited horses that are gaining in popularity with the recreational rider, especially those with joint and back problems. Gaited horses have more gaits than the walk, trot, and canter common to most horses. These in-between gaits are extremely comfortable and don't jostle the rider around much. (Photo © Bob Langrish)

perform the running walk at almost 30 mph! Icelandics also use the traditional walk, trot, and canter.

PASO FINO

The Paso Fino is the American version of a horse called the Peruvian Paso. In Argentina the Paso Fino is called the Criollo. These horses are descendents of Spanish horses, and Spanish conquistadors used them as remounts in the New World. With the help of early sixteenth-century explorers such as Hernando Cortez and Diego de Velasquez, who traveled on Paso Finos, the horses became known in places such as Puerto Rico, Cuba, Colombia, Panama, and Mexico.

The Paso Fino has a four-beat lateral gait, as opposed to the more common movement where each front foot moves in tandem with the opposite back foot. The gait has three phases—the paso fino, paso corto, and paso largo; the corto is the working gait for trail riding. Riders remain flat in their seats, even at significant speeds. Paso Finos also walk and canter, both of which come naturally to the horse and are not "trained" gaits.

The Paso Fino is a small horse, averaging just under 15 hands. They are used for carriage driving as well as for bird hunting; their short stature makes them easy to mount and dismount frequently.

ROCKY MOUNTAIN HORSE

The Rocky Mountain Horse, or pony, as it is sometimes called, is a relative newcomer on the horse breed scene; its registry just opened in 1986. The founding of this interesting breed of American horse is attributed to Sam Tuttle of Stout Springs, Kentucky. Their four-beat gait made them naturally comfortable to ride and perfect for clambering around the Appalachian foothills.

These horses are not only beautiful, typically sporting chocolate brown coats and flaxen manes and tails, but they also have all the characteristics of a perfect family horse. They are medium height,

sure footed, easy to keep, gentle in nature, easy to ride, and have great endurance.

The Rocky Mountain Horse Association is concerned with preserving the breed. If a horse is to be registered with the association, its sire and dam must meet very strict guidelines prior to breeding.

The Rocky Mountain Horse is becoming more popular and now has representation at the Kentucky Horse Park. The breed can be found in all parts of the country.

TENNESSEE WALKING HORSE

This classic gaited horse was originally cobbled together from a mix of the Narragansett Pacer, Thoroughbred, Morgan, Standardbred, and Saddlebred horses. Tennessee Walkers are used extensively as driving horses, but it is their unique, comfortable gait that made them the favorite saddle horse of country doctors, traveling preachers, plantation owners, and others who needed to cover a lot of ground and spent many hours in the saddle.

Rocky Mountain Horse

The Rocky Mountain Horse is relatively new to the horse breed scene. Typically a beautiful chocolate brown color with a flaxen mane and tail, the sturdy Rocky Mountain Horse now has its own association that is dedicated to preserving the breed. (Photo © Bob Langrish)

Tennessee Walking Horse

The Tennessee Walking Horse is another gaited breed that makes a sturdy and comfortable mount for the recreational rider. (Photo courtesy the Tennessee Walking Horse Breeders and Exhibitors Association)

One of the Tennessee Walker's gaits, like the Icelandic, is the "running walk," which is not a trained gait but a natural inherited one. In the running walk the horse overstrides, planting its hind foot ahead of the footprint left behind by its front foot. (Horses typically have a stride known as tracking, where a hind foot steps in the footprint of the front foot.) The Tennessee Walker swings its head noticeably in rhythm with the walk, moving its ears and sometimes even clacking its teeth. The Tennessee Walker is also known for two other unusual gaits—the "flat-foot walk" and the "rocking chair" canter.

Aside from being extremely comfortable to ride, the Tennessee Walking Horses are known for their hardiness and good health. They are typically black, al-though they can be any of the traditional horse coat colorings. They usually stand between 15 and 16 hands tall.

Ponies

Ponies—a type of equine that is limited to under 14.2 hands in size—are experiencing a great resurgence in popularity, as more of the larger pony breeds are used by adults as performance animals. These sturdy little mounts tend to be easier to keep than their larger counterparts, and they often have personality to spare.

CONNEMARA

The Connemara pony originated along the rocky western coast of Ireland, where the hardy breed lived off poor pasture in harsh weather. The Connemara was

Connemara

The Connemara is one of many pony breeds that originated in the United Kingdom. This sturdy, Irish large pony breed is known for being exceptionally hardy. Connemaras have become popular show and jumping ponies for young riders in the United States. (Photo © Bob Langrish)

refined through breeding with Arabian and Spanish horses.

By the turn of the twentieth century, many Connemara ponies were stabled instead of living in the wild. Stabling created an inferior, less hardy breed. In the 1920s, in an effort to reverse this trend, some Irish owners picked out a dozen high-quality Connemaras and allowed them to live and breed in the wild, where the hardiest survived and reproduced. The Connemara Pony Breeders' Society was established in Ireland 1923 and the studbook set up in 1926.

The Connemara stands between 12.2 and 14.2 hands. It is most often grey in color, but may also be black, bay, and brown. Connemaras are considered great performance ponies, excelling as hunters and jumpers, but they also compete in dressage, distance trail riding, and under harness.

EXMOOR

The Exmoor pony is one of the oldest of what are known as the British Mountain Ponies and the current specimens have not changed much from their prehistoric origins. The Exmoor pony has a seventh molar, a characteristic found in no other equine. Other unique features enabled the breed to withstand the harsh climate of the Exmoor region. It has a hooded eye for protection against wind and rain, and it has a "snow-chute" or "ice tail," a tuft of hair at the top of the tail that wicks

Exmoor
With a seventh molar and other physical characteristics unique to its breed, the Exmoor is a sturdy pony that has not changed much from its prehistoric origins. (Photo courtesy the Exmoor Pony Enthusiasts)

water and snow away from its body. This tail hair sheds in the summer and regrows again each fall. Exmoors are always bay in color and have lighter hair around their eyes and at their muzzles. They stand between 11.2 and 12.3 hands and weigh around 750 pounds.

Exmoors were the chariot-pulling ponies of the Bronze Age, but eventually became saddle horses capable of carrying full-grown men. They are now used in almost all performance categories and have an uncanny jumping ability. Exmoors have been on the rare breed list and were first imported into Canada in the 1950s. It is becoming a more popular breed in Canada and the United States alike.

"My Little Pony" Is Not a Baby Horse

A pony is not a baby horse. A baby horse is called a "foal." A female baby horse is a "filly," and a male baby horse is a "colt." The foal still nursing its mother is a "suckling"; when it is weaned from its mother, usually between four and six months of age, it is referred to as a "weanling." At a year it is a "yearling," but any young horse is often still called a colt or a filly until it is fully mature, anywhere from three to eight years old or perhaps, in fillies, after they have produced their first foal. Often all young horses are called colts, for convenience's sake.

Although a strict definition of a pony is that it must be under 14.2 hands, a small-sized horse is not a pony. Ponies are very specific breeds of horses (such as Shetland, Welsh Cob, or Connemara), and their diminutive size is inherent to their breed.

Fell

This Fell Pony was the 2002 Champion at the Fell Pony Society Show in the United Kingdom. These sturdy ponies were once almost exclusively used as pack animals but today are becoming increasingly popular as riding ponies. (© MJ Gould-Earley, courtesy of Fell Pony Society of North America, Inc.)

FELL

These sturdy black ponies originated in northern England and are a bit smaller and lighter than their close cousin, the Dales pony. Fell ponies were used traditionally as pack ponies, but they were also used for riding and driving. Today it is common to cross the Fell with other breeds to create great performance ponies. The Fell was a foundation breed for creating the Hackney pony. Fell ponies never exceed 14 hands, and they are almost always black, although brown, bay, and grey are rare but acceptable colors.

FJORD

The Norwegian Fjord bears a remarkable resemblance to the ancient Asian Wild Horse. It is a creamy dun color with a dorsal stripe down its back, and it typically has zebra striping on its legs. The Fjords' mane and tail are unique, standing erect like their wild ancestors' and having silver on the outside with black down the middle. Fjord owners groom these manes to follow the arch of the pony's crested neck, accentuating the black stripe.

Fjords were the horse of choice for the Vikings, who used them in "horse fighting,"

a sport similar to cockfighting. Fjords stand between 13 and 14 hands and are strongly muscled and stocky. Today they are used for plowing, packing, and riding.

HAFLINGER

The beautiful little Haflinger originated in the village of Hafling, Austria (now part of Italy). The Haflinger breed began in 1874 with the birth of the founding stallion, named 249 Folie, bred from a Tyrolean mare and a half-Arabian stallion. All Haflingers trace back to 249 Folie.

The Haflinger is palomino in color with a creamy golden body and flaxen

Fjord

It is unusual to see a Fjord with a blanket on as these ponies are exceptionally well suited to even the harshest climates and typically prefer little if any shelter. Their unusual straight mane, which is white on either side with a chocolate stripe down the middle, makes them just cute as can be. (Shutterstock Photo)

mane and tail. It stands around 13.3 hands and has a more refined action than the standard draft pony. Haflingers are known to be extremely sound and sturdy, befitting a pony originating in a mountainous region.

The Haflinger arrived in North America in 1958, and it is a popular breed in the United States and Canada today. Haflingers are used for riding and driving and are particularly popular for forestry work.

Welsh Cob and Pony

Welsh ponies come also in a smaller size known as a "cob." They are versatile ponies, having been used in coal mines, to haul military equipment, and for mail delivery. (Photo © Bob Langrish)

SHETLAND

The Shetland is what almost every child dreams of when they proclaim they want a pony. The Shetland, which originated on the Shetland Islands, is thought to be the oldest breed of horse in Great Britain. They were domesticated by Islanders to haul peat for fuel and seaweed for fertilizer.

For its size, the Shetland is considered one of the strongest of the equine species. These ponies were used extensively to haul coal cars. Some spent their entire lives, from birth to death, in coal mines and were exported to the United States to do the same.

The American Shetland, a cross between the Shetland and the Hackney pony, is a more refined pony. The Pony of the Americas is a Shetland crossed with the Appaloosa.

WELSH COB AND PONY

The Welsh Pony and smaller Welsh Cob hail from Wales, where they thrived on rough terrain and sparse vegetation. The Welsh Pony has some Arabian in its history, and today it is often crossed with other breeds, especially the Thoroughbred. Welsh Ponies pulled chariots, worked in coal mines, hauled heavy guns and military equipment over mountain terrain, and delivered the mail. They escaped Henry VII's call to destroy all horses under 15 hands, and they

emerged a versatile and people-loving breed of pony.

The Welsh Pony was imported to the United States in the 1880s, and the U.S. breed society for the Welsh Pony was established in 1907. Any color is acceptable, although most individuals are bay, brown, or black. They have spectacular hind-limb action and can cover good ground at a trot. The society registers Welsh Ponies in four sections, A through D, according to different height restrictions. Section D, for Welsh Cobs, starts at 13.2 hands and has no upper height limit.

Shetland

The Shetland has always been thought of as a fat little pony, and their compact size made them perfect candidates for a life in the coal mines, both in their native Shetland Islands and in the United States. The breed in the United States today has branched out to a more refined pony. (Photo © Bob Langrish)

Chapter Four

A Horse Is a Horse Is a Horse:

Equine Behavior in a Nutshell

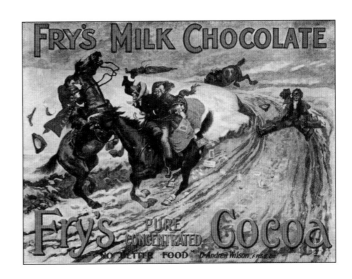

Colts at Play in Montana

Young horses love to play, particularly the colts. They rear and kick and bite and run around in what seems like preparation for the role they would take in the wild as the herd stallion. Fillies don't seem to do quite as much roughhousing. Their play tends more toward mutual grooming and some running around, but not the rough-and-tumble activities in which colts engage. (Photo © Alan & Sandy Carey)

Fry's Milk Chocolate Ad

The horses appear to be behaving badly in this early 1900s advertisement for Fry's Milk Chocolate and Pure Concentrated Cocoa.

F or horse owners, horse behavior is the most intriguing and most frustrating part of having them around. Unless you spend some time learning about the horse's general makeup, you will go crazy trying to understand why horses do the things they do. To the uninitiated, horse behavior can seem a bit strange.

As a case in point, a wild tom turkey came wandering up to our horse area one day, and my husband observed the horses' reaction. All five horses lined up along the fenceline, snorting and wide-eyed. When my husband told the story, he chuckled and remarked, "Five thousand pounds of horse afraid of a little old turkey." But the horses, which are very comfortable in their turnout area, do not see turkeys often, so they were startled and intrigued by the visitor. It did not take them too long to realize that the turkey was not a threat, and once they did, they went about their usual business.

Wild Horses

Wild horse bands still roam small areas in America. The bands are well organized with a lead mare, a protective stallion, his harem of breeding mares, and young animals that haven't yet left to join another band or form their own. (Shutterstock Photo)

Most horses grow accustomed to cars whizzing by when you ride them on a road; once they are comfortable with that, you need to be careful that something on the side of the road—a lunging dog or a blowing piece of paper—doesn't cause them to jump out into the road in front of a car. This contradictory behavior is the type of thing that makes people not familiar with horses look at you funny when you talk about horse behavior as if it makes sense.

Wild Horses

Horse behavior, like horse evolution, is pretty well studied. Much of the formal research on horses is based on the study of wild herds, which in the United States today means the bands of horses that live on federally owned, open range land and have little or no contact with humans. The horses are confined, but that confinement extends across thousands of acres. Observation of these herds has led to an understanding of the roles played by different members of the herd.

The herd dynamic is vital to a social animal like the horse. This sense of order protects horses from harm, keeps them nourished, and ensures propagation. The herd's many members are all key players in their own right.

THE STALLION

A relatively young, vigorous male horse keeps vigil over a band of females that are his and his alone to breed. He defends his mares against other stallions that are looking to collect a harem of their own. The stallion also warns of encroaching dangers and fends off predators, allowing the rest of the herd to escape to safer ground.

THE LEAD MARE

Although the stallion's harem comprises as many mares as he can gather and control, one mare is considered the boss. She is the horse that leads the herd to grazing lands and watering holes, decides where

The Stallion

Contrary to popular belief, this wild stallion is not the leader of his band. Where the band goes and when is decided by a mare; the stallion breeds receptive mares and defends the herd against danger. (Shutterstock Photo)

Earned Stripes

Three species of zebra—Equus burchelli, grevyi, and zebra—survived evolution to become part of recorded history. Despite the focus of the fun 2005 movie, *Racing Stripes*, no zebra is considered well suited for riding, both for conformational and behavioral reasons. (Shutterstock Photo)

the herd will go at any given time, and basically determines who in the herd will stand where and when. Horse herds have a pecking order of influence, and it all starts here with the lead mare.

OTHER MARES

Propagation is the stallion's main objective, and the more mares he has in his harem, the more successfully he propagates. The mares of the herd are his to breed, but the stallion's harem is limited by the number of mares he is capable of defending against young stallions looking to develop their own harems.

COLTS

Male offspring are allowed to remain with the herd until they come of breeding age and become competition for the stallion. They are then driven out of the herd, where they often join other colts to form "bachelor bands." These small herds of young males travel together, each looking to create his own band of mares.

One interesting key difference between domestic and wild horses is that there are no geldings (neutered males) in the wild herd; in other words, there are no members of the wild horse herd that are not concerned with reproduction, as there are in the domestic herd. For this reason, geldings often get along peaceably with all members of a domestic horse herd, provided the other horses are well socialized. (Some geldings still exhibit a sex drive, but they usually don't fully act upon it.)

FILLIES

The female offspring either remain with the herd to be bred by their own sire, the stallion of the herd, or they are stolen from the herd by a bachelor colt as he creates his own harem.

In a horse herd, all members except the lead mare have horses above and below them in the pecking order (the stallion ranking a close second to the lead mare). All members of the herd know their places, allowing for the herd to function efficiently for the health and safety of all concerned. That said, the pecking order

Przewalski's Horse

Today the only horse that can be traced straight back to prehistoric times is Przewalski's horse. It was named after the Russian naturalist Colonel Nikolai Przewalski (pronounced "Persia-VAL-skee"), who discovered the horse in Southwest Mongolia in 1879.

The Przewalski's horse stands at a pony-sized 12 to 14 hands. It is dun colored with a dorsal stripe, with zebralike stripes on its legs and a light-colored muzzle. Its mane grows upright and does not flop over, no matter how long it gets.

Przewalski's horse has sixty chromosomes, while the modern domestic horse has sixty-four, a genetic difference leading many to dispute claims that the Przewalski's horse is a direct ancestor of the modern horse.

Although thought to be the last remaining wild horse, no Przewalski's horses have been seen in the wild since the late 1960s. A couple of times in the 1900s, Przewalski's horses were caught to disperse to zoos around the world, but many did not survive the lengthy boat trip to their new home or they arrived in such poor condition that they died soon after the journey. In 1979, the Foundation for the Preservation and Protection of Przewalski's Horse began to purchase zoo animals in order to re-introduce them to the wild. The preservation of the Przewalski's horse and its endangered natural habitat, the steppe, is underway.

Horses on the Run

Wild horses run full speed ahead during a round-up in Wyoming. (Photo © Rita Summers)

Przewalski's Horse

Thought to be the truest ancient species related to the modern horse, Przewalski's is currently only found in captivity. Efforts to reinvigorate their habitat, the Russian steppes, are coinciding with efforts to save the species. (Shutterstock Photo)

Beautiful Pastures

Horses typically get along well and sort out the pecking order without more than a bite mark or two if given plenty of space in which to roam. Pastures are usually divided by fencing and rotated regularly to allow one area to "rest" and regrow. This also helps to keep parasite infestation down. (Shutterstock Photo)

isn't static. Horses are always trying to move up, or they may move down as they age or become injured.

Domestic Horses

Although wild behaviors are certainly inherent in our backyard horses, domestication has transformed the horse into a bit of a different animal—my theory is that the contemporary domestic horse is becoming a new species altogether, similar to the difference between a wolf and a dog, but I have no scientific research to back up that theory.

Just having to learn to incorporate a nonspecies member—a human—into the dynamics of the herd makes a huge difference in the behavior of the domesticated horse. I keep my horses in a pretty open environment; they are rarely confined to stalls. That means I feed five loose horses every day. I realize it is important for my safety that these horses understand boundaries while I am in their area, especially when I have food in my hands. Their intention is not, of course, to hurt me. Each of them is focused on getting their feed in the appropriate order and quantity afforded them by their status in the herd. But if one decides to run another off, and I am in the midst of bared teeth, thundering legs, and flying hooves, I am going to get hurt. So I have had to establish rules about not roughing up the food delivery person.

In the beginning I had to be pretty assertive, perhaps even aggressive, to make sure the horses understood the boundaries. Now I have to reinforce the rules on occasion; many horses will constantly test their herd status, and I always have to re-introduce the rules when a new horse enters the herd. I don't believe, although some do, that I have to become part of the herd or that I have to be the "alpha" horse, as happens in the wild. (I'm quite certain horses aren't so stupid as to think I am another horse.) But I do have to establish my particular role within the herd. For horses, how to incorporate a human into their herd is not something that comes naturally; it is one of the learned behaviors that sets domestic horses apart from their wild counterparts.

Another huge influence on the domestic horse is confinement. Confining a horse to a stall goes against the horse's natural way of life. Confinement can cause many health and behavior problems that can be annoying and dangerous to humans.

Horses are big animals and every bodily function—from generating sufficient body warmth to properly digesting food, to ensuring adequate blood circulation in their feet and legs—is designed to function best with constant movement.

Ruminants such as cows, sheep, and goats eat large amounts of food as fast as possible then find a safe place to lie down and allow the food to travel through their complex digestive system. These animals have a holding tank called the rumen that stores and begins to break down some of the food, while food continues to run through the three other stomachs that make up the ruminant digestive tract.

Horses, on the other hand, have very small stomachs and very simple digestive systems—in some ways too simple for their large bodies. The horse was designed to eat, move, eat, move, eat, move. Through grazing for their food, digestion takes place gradually and constantly, so food is running straight through their system at

Good Grazing

Good grazing in open pasture is the best thing for a horse both physically and mentally. Roam and eat, eat and roam is what they are designed to do! (© Norvia Behling)

81

Horse May Bite

Without fingers, horses naturally use their mouths to investigate things. Humans often encourage horses to bite accidentally by feeding them treats by hand, by touching a horse on the nose, or even by moving away from the horse that's behaving menacingly (status in the herd is determined by who moves whom). The pounds-per-square-inch pressure delivered by a horse's huge mandibles can bite off a human finger pretty easily. (Shutterstock Photo)

all times—the human horsekeeper could imitate this by standing at the stall door and delivering small amounts of hay every half hour, something few people have time for or are willing to do. Regurgitation is not part of the equine digestive process as it is with ruminants; a horse is anatomically incapable of regurgitating food, which is one of the reasons that colic is such a problem for horses. So when a horse eats something, it either digests the nutritious stuff and passes the waste products out the other end or what it ate stays somewhere in the system, causing problems for the animal.

Bad Behavior

One of the main things that makes domestic horses increasingly different from their wild ancestors is that domestication has required them to live under conditions that make their care and use convenient for humans. And what's most convenient for humans is to confine horses in or at least close to the barn. The convenience of confining a horse, however, means humans have to deal with some frustrating, complicated, sometimes dangerous, and even sad behavioral issues, things that no wild horse would ever do. These so-called stable vices are seen regularly with backyard pet horses, and they are seen in alarmingly graphic fashion in racehorses and other high-level performance horses.

Walk through any racehorse stable and you will almost definitely see dramatic examples of:

- weaving, where a horse stands at its stall door and endlessly shifts back and forth from one front foot to the other

- cribbing, where a horse grips its top teeth on the edge of a door or fence board or feed bucket, pulls back, and lets out a grunt

New Toy

Like children who prefer the box the toy came in, horses seem to enjoy playing with the hay and water buckets. (Photo by Cheryl Kimball)

- lunging at the doorway as people walk past

- raking teeth down the sides of the wall or the rungs on the stall grating

- incessantly walking in circles around the stall

Performance horses are fed huge amounts of food to make them grow faster than nature intended (those big horses running the Kentucky Derby are just three-year-olds) and give them the energy and stamina they need to perform. But in an attempt to preserve that energy for the race and to ensure the horses don't injure themselves, racehorses, for example, spend as much as twenty-three hours of each day in a stall. That's like packing your teenaged son full of food and locking him in his room most of the time. Give that a try and see how it works!

Other, more dangerous behaviors include kicking and biting. A horse kicks at something for one reason: It feels threatened. If it is confined and cannot flee—typically a horse's first choice when threatened—it will kick out. Some horses are more prone to kicking than others. A horse almost always gives signals when it is about to kick; it may put its ears back, shake its head, twitch its tail, or shift its weight. But for the unaware or inexperienced person, sometimes the kick can be unexpected.

"Stella!"

Horse Play

Horses have been the focus of many cartoons in *The New Yorker* over the years. This particular cartoon appeared in the March 24, 2003 issue. (Photo used courtesy of *The New Yorker*)

Horsing Around

Sometimes horses just seem to be loving life. (Photo by Gena McGrath)

A horse's ability to feel comfortable "switching eyes" without startling is a key component for safer interactions with humans. Take, for instance, a person walking behind a horse with a wheelbarrow. Out of its left eye, the horse sees that person go behind it. When the person walks farther and the horse suddenly picks up the wheelbarrow out of its right eye, the wheelbarrow may startle the horse and it may kick out. And since the wheelbarrow has already come into the horse's field of vision, the person pushing the wheelbarrow is the one that gets kicked.

Some horses switch eyes without a problem right from the start; others need to get a few lessons to help them learn to switch eyes and allow someone to walk behind them safely. A good horse handler will teach a horse early on to be comfort-able switching eyes since this is a critical safety component during those first few rides when the horse sees the rider on its back for the first time.

Lastly, horses can be impossible to catch if they don't want to be caught, even when in a stall with a halter on. Few people are going to readily confront a horse when it puts its head in the far corner of the stall and turns its hind end toward the door the moment a person goes into the stall to retrieve it. Horses learn this technique and become very good at the hard-to-catch game—you can use up a good portion of the time you have to ride trying to get a lead rope (the equine equivalent of a dog leash) on an evasive horse. It helps to occasionally catch your horse for some reason other than going for a ride—maybe just to give it a nice scratch on the shoulder or under the chin, to brush it even just in the paddock or stall, or to bring it out for a little grazing in a lush part of the lawn.

Horse Play

Every day at around four in the afternoon, my two colts—now ages three and four—begin to play. It starts innocently enough, usually with what I call "the merry go 'round," where they stand head to tail, and one bites the other in the tender part of the flank. The bitten one then tucks his tail, scoots a few feet, and bites his pal in the flank. The first colt then tucks his tail, and around and around they go—bite, tuck, scoot, bite, tuck, scoot—until they are almost dragging their rear ends along the ground. I've always enjoyed watching them, but I never realized how common their different games are until I heard other people telling stories about their own colts, even describing this particular game as looking like carousel horses.

There are other regular colt games as well. "Face fighting," where two colts stand almost perfectly still and bat at each other with their heads and maybe get in a few nips, is popular; it seems when horses put a fence between them, face fighting is that much more fun. Grabbing the crest of the neck and hanging on while the horse being bitten tries to flee is apparently quite entertaining as well.

Males seem to love games more than females. I have consistently heard people who raise horses say that the females just don't play much, even as youngsters. *The Merck Veterinary Manual* backs up this anecdotal evidence: "There are sex differences in play; colts play more than fillies and play different games than do fillies. Colt games focus more on fighting and mounting, while filly games focus on running and mutual grooming."

It would seem that mares do not need the skills that the colts' games develop; the assumption is that all of this play fighting prepares the colt for the herd dynamic and the time when he will chal-

lenge a stallion for control of a harem or defend his own harem against a challenging younger male. If the colts' foolishness gets too close to either of my adult mares, they display their disdain with flattened ears, bobbing heads, and, if necessary, a kick or charge.

If my seventeen-year-old gelding is any indication, boys will be boys, even beyond their youth. He gets right in there with the young fellows and plays the boy horse games. Occasionally the three males run at full speed around the pasture. Whatever the underlying reason for their behavior, any observer can have little doubt that the games are great fun and release a lot of the colts' boundless energy.

Face Fighting

So-called "face fighting" is a common type of play for horses, especially young colts. My teenage gelding and his four-year-old pasture mate seem to especially like a good face fight with a fence in between them; perhaps this is their way of making sure the older horse doesn't get too rough and hurt the younger one. (Photo © Daniel Johnson)

I go about looking at horses and cattle. They eat grass, make love, work when they have to, bear their young. I am sick with envy of them.
–Sherwood Anderson

Wait Your Turn

The horse on the left is waiting patiently to see if the boss horse of the herd will allow her to join the feed pile. The horse eating the hay sends subtle signals that the other horse is not welcome. (Photo by Cheryl Kimball)

Eating Behaviors

Feeding time instigates a unique set of behaviors, many annoying, some dangerous, others just plain curious. My older gelding sticks his head in the plastic feeder that hangs on the fence and rings it like a dinner bell. The eight-year-old Arabian mare stands at the hayrack and uses her teeth to twang the lip of the hard rubber tub like a musical instrument. Ruby, my twelve-year-old Quarter Horse mare, stands at her feed bucket, puts her nose to the ground, and paws when I am on my way to feed her. I recall that her mother did this, so it is most likely a learned behavior.

I always considered Ruby's behavior yet another sign of her impatience and have found it annoying, much like having the kids pound their forks on the table while their parents prepare dinner. As if anyone would put up with that. I tried for years to break her of this pawing, mostly by refusing to deposit the feed in the bucket until she stopped. But she paws and paws and paws when I am not yet in sight; I have little ability to influence this behavior until I am actually at her feed tub. She has come to learn that I will not deposit the food into her bucket until her head is up and all four feet are on the ground, but that does not stop the pawing during food preparation

time. A few years ago I made a discovery that made me think I will never cure her of this habit.

For two years, my husband and I rented a house on the Wisconsin/Minnesota border. Our neighbor turned his broodmares out on the twenty-one-acre pasture beside and behind our house. On moonlit nights in the middle of the frigid Upper Midwest winter, I could see those mares behind my house pawing in the snow trying to uncover some dried up old blade of grass. Their behavior reminded me of Ruby, who not only paws around feeding time but also stops to sniff where she has pawed. It is as if some ingrained instinct requires her to search for her food even though it comes like clockwork at feeding time. I have come to believe that Ruby has taken an instinct and turned it into a stable vice. Horses also paw for reasons other than to search for food in deep snow. They will paw a hole in the ice to get water or to make the hole larger, to dig up roots to eat, and to fluff up a dirt area to roll in.

Another relatively common food-related behavior is "hay dunking," which is when horses bring a mouthful of hay to the water bucket, slop the hay around in the water, and eat it wet. Hay dunking can make a mess of the watering tub, but it is probably more of a good thing than a bad thing. There are a couple of reasons horses may become hay dunkers.

First, horses were not meant to eat the dried, baled grass we call hay. Their digestive systems were designed to thrive on live grass, which provides a great amount of moisture. Consuming hay without drinking water can lead to major digestive problems, including what is known as "impaction colic," where the digested food is so dry it simply gets stuck in the plumbing. Undereducated horse owners who think that eating snow in the winter provides the horse with enough moisture can end up with a horse with major medical problems. Horses drink 10 to 15 gallons of water a day. Try melting what you think is a huge amount of snow sometime and see how little water it amounts to.

Besides common digestive problems, horses also have sensitive respiratory systems. It is impossible to eat dry hay and not encounter some level of dust, but dusty, moldy hay can cause horses a lifetime of breathing problems generically known as "heaves." Horses with heaves often need to eat hay that has been intentionally soaked in a bucket for a half hour or so before it is fed to them. Anyone who has to soak their horse's hay before every feeding wishes the horse would learn to be a dunker!

Affection

Whether or not horses show affection is a debatable question. It's clear that horses seek each other's company. Horses in a

Quenching a Mighty Thirst
An adult horse drinks between ten and fifteen gallons of water a day. Horses must have access to water all the time, as hydration is key in regulating their body temperature. Eating snow in winter provides nowhere near enough water. Many horse owners use electrically heated buckets like this one to keep the water free of ice in below-freezing temperatures. (Photo by Cheryl Kimball)

There is something about the outside of a horse that is good for the inside of a man.
–Winston Churchill

A Sign of Affection?
These two horses look as if they are being affectionate, but mutual grooming and scratching is a common horse activity, especially among fillies. (Photo by Robert Sarosiek, Shutterstock)

A Wink and a Smile
Who knows exactly what this horse's intention is, but horses (such as this one in a zoo) who are confined and confronted a lot by people not sensitive to horses become adept at appearing to be menacing. (Shutterstock photo)

If you sit on a sturdy fence surrounding a horse pasture, a horse may walk over and eventually end up with its head resting in your lap.

But all of these things can be explained as having more practical purposes than mere affection. Horses that hang out together help swish flies away from each other in summer; often you can see two horses standing nose-to-tail in the summer, using each other's tails to flick flies off the other's face and chest. In the winter, horses provide each other with warmth and windbreaks.

Horses do best in familiar settings, so what may appear to be mourning the death of a particular stable companion is perhaps just being out of sorts with, well, things being out of sorts. The mourning-like behavior would likely vanish quickly if the horse were provided another companion with which it also got along well.

The mare that seems to be showing affection by always coming near me when I enter her corral is most likely just well tuned to the fact that I can, and more importantly, will scratch her in places she cannot reach herself.

herd will often hang out with the same horse or group of horses. That is most likely because the hierarchical structure makes this group of horses the ones they get along with the best. And horses are almost always looking to simply get along. There are stories about horses that appear to mourn after the death or removal of a horse with whom they've lived, implying that there might be feelings of affection among horses.

As for affection with people, it is clear that horses that have good experience with humans trust and enjoy people and seem to like interacting with people. If I go out into the corral with my horses, my favorite mare will always come over and stand by me, edging closer and closer until I can't help but rub and scratch her.

Curiosity

One of the most surprising behaviors that horses exhibit is an immense curiosity. Put something new in a horse's corral, and you won't have to wait long for the horse to come check it out. People who don't have much personal contact with horses are often amazed by this behavior. I was too until I started seeing it firsthand.

Shortly after I brought my first two horses to our farm, my husband and I were making a repair in Bud and Ruby's turnout area. We used a wheelbarrow to carry in the requisite tools and supplies. The horses would get very close to what we were doing, as if it was important for them to know what was going on in their area. We found that we had to keep rescuing things they would snatch from the wheelbarrow. I finally had to ward them off so Jack could pound in a nail without smacking a horse's nose on the backstroke of the hammer.

One spring I hired a contractor to do some fence work for me. When I returned home one day after work, he asked me to rescue his sweatshirt from the middle of the horse pasture. He had tossed it on the fence and looked up moments later and see one of the horses walking away with it.

My father-in-law, Dave, does a lot of photography. To my great fortune, he finds the horses fascinating and spends quite a bit of time photographing them when he visits the farm. On one visit, Dave was standing near the fence when my young Morgan-Quarter Horse colt reached over and grabbed his coat. Bugsy didn't bite, didn't lunge, just wadded up a bit of sleeve in his mouth and then he let

Nosy Horse
Horses are so curious it can be hard to take pictures of them! (Photo by Cheryl Kimball)

Scratchin' That Itch
Rolling is a behavior horses do for many reasons including covering themselves with dust to deter flies, scratching an itchy spot, trying to relieve stomach pain, or just for the sheer fun of it. A horse that can roll completely from one side to the other without standing up is said to be worth more money than one that has to roll on one side, stand up, then drop to the other side. (Shutterstock photo)

89

a.

b.

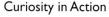

c.

d.

Curiosity in Action

[a]Each spring during a late snowfall I make the horses some snowmen to play with.

[b]They watch me the whole time and when I finally open the gate they are cautiously curious to investigate.

[c]Danger, run away! A limb snapped, a car backfired, or something happened to make them suspicious of these intruders.

[d]Once they understand that the snowmen are not only harmless but also are bearing hay for hair, carrot noses, apples for eyes, and horse treat smiles, the snowmen do not last long! (Photos by Cheryl Kimball)

go. "Why did he do that?" my father-in-law asked. I guess because he was curious about how Dave's coat might taste.

One explanation for this high level of curiosity may be the need for a prey animal to completely understand the level of danger represented by anything in its "flight zone." The flight zone is the number of feet a prey animal will allow between itself and a potential predator before it is hardwired to flee. Deer have a large flight zone; something unknown usually can't get too close before the deer takes off. Moose have a smaller flight zone; strange things can typically get a little closer to a moose than a deer, perhaps

because the moose's single stride takes it a lot farther than a deer's does. A horse's flight zone is probably more like a deer's, but in the safety of the horses' known environment—their everyday turnout area near their home barn—they can be more curious than afraid.

Riders can get this curiosity working for them from the saddle. By exposing a horse to potentially scary things and encouraging their curiosity, riders can attempt to make their mount's flight zone quite small and thus make many riding problems disappear.

The Education of a Horse

The group of riders I associate with think in terms of *educating* horses, not *training* them. The difference is at once huge and subtle.

Training mostly employs a useful if overused tool called "conditioned response." Conditioned-response training is more like teaching a horse tricks than actually educating them. You can teach a horse to "count" to ten, but it really can't count. You set up a condition, and every time that condition occurs, the horse will respond in the same way.

When you educate a horse, you teach the horse to think. A horse that is encouraged to think things through is more likely to provide a safe ride.

For example, pick up and hold taut the reins of a young horse newly started under saddle to ask it to back up; few horses will automatically step backward, since backing up is not a movement that a horse uses much in the wild. Most will move their head from side to side or up in the air to relieve the pressure of the bit against the corners of their mouth. Horses learn what's expected of them by what happens when the pressure is released. A horse needs an almost immediate response in order to connect the release of pressure with what it did, so in educating horses, the rider or handler must have incredibly good timing. In the case of the young horse backing up, the rider waits for even the slightest shift of the horse's body weight backward and relieves the pressure of the bit. When the rider repeats this exercise a few times, the horse will begin to shift its weight at the slightest pressure, and by then the pressure may even come from your seat not the reins/bit. Allowing the horse to search for the correct answer helps them respond with thoughtfulness.

This release of pressure can be used in almost every aspect of educating the horse. A horse that is not allowed to use its brain or a horse with a rider or handler who sends mixed messages will simply

Professor Crocker's Educated Horses

Horses are astute observers and pick up on the subtlest visual cues. In any book on horse behavior you will read the story of Clever Hans. In the late 1800s, his owner, a European professor, taught Clever Hans to "do math," and the horse became quite celebrated. The professor would give Hans a math problem, and the horse would count out the correct answer with his front foot, receiving a sugar cube treat for his skill. Scientists were skeptical of Hans's ability, but when they gave Hans math problems themselves, he always answered correctly. Finally, scientists were able to solve the mystery when they asked the professor to leave the room. It turned out Hans was picking up on the twitch of the professor's eyebrow. The professor had trained Hans to paw each time the man raised his eyebrow. Hans was clever all right, but not necessarily in arithmetic.

Left: Professor Crocker's Educated Horses

Horses taught to do tricks (even ones that make them seem to be able to do math or answer complex questions) have been making money for humans for hundreds of years. (Photo used courtesy of the Library of Congress Print and Photographs Division)

Tips on Handling Young Ones

Clinician Bryan Neubert demonstrates how he would work to make a couple skittish weanlings easier to handle. The horse attached to the lead rope was already pretty comfortable with humans. The other horse was not, so the clinician scratches an itchy spot to let the horse see that humans can be good to have around. (Photo by Rick Larsen)

check out. Rent-by-the-hour trail horses are safe for anyone to ride because the horses have learned not to listen to the signals of the rider; those inconsistent signals are mostly meaningless to them. And these horses live a great life as long as they follow their buddies along a set trail. Take them out of that environment, and they will usually not be as easy for the inexperienced rider to handle.

Starting Young Horses Under Saddle

Cowboys will have a string of horses to use for ranch work and will pick among them according to the horses' age, education,

and the job at hand. Big ranches usually have a wrangler or two to train young horses for riding but the cowboy typically picks up the responsibility for the horse's education after the initial training.

The Old West was notoriously hard on horses, and the traditional methods for training young stock for the saddle were no exception. The term "breaking" came about because the training had a real tendency to break the horse's spirit—at times even breaking the horse physically, resulting in the horse's tragic death or an injury that made the horse unusable.

Horsemanship has moved toward referring to this part of a horse's education as "starting a horse under saddle" or "colt starting" ("colts" being the generic term often used for young horses, whether they are male or female). This evolution is, thankfully, more than just semantics—it is a real shift in training methods. Even though stock-type horses used in ranch work are pretty much full sized and filled out by the time they are two years old, most horses aren't truly mature—with bone growth plates hardened, especially in the knees—until they are four or five. (Arabians are notoriously slow to grow and are not considered fully mature until almost eight. They also tend to have a longer lifespan, which, for most horses, averages around twenty-four years old.) In the 1800s, a ranch horse may not have been started under saddle until it was three or more, basically when the horse was old enough and sturdy enough to handle a day's work. Eventually riders began to start horses under saddle at age two (especially racehorses but that is a completely different training process). As a result these horses often have a shorter useable lifespan and their joints break down sooner than they ordinarily would. Horses are started in their working life a little later than they used to be, perhaps because we use horses mostly for leisure rather than for real work these days. And, educating a horse to the saddle has come to involve working with the horse's natural instincts.

One key element of using a horse's instincts—and a key difference from the old breaking days—is to allow the horse freedom of movement. A horse's instinct is to flee danger. Strap something onto its back for the first time, and it wants to run. Instead of snubbing a horse to a post with a rope, getting the saddle on as best you can, and letting the horse fight it out until he's exhausted, gets hurt, or plumb gives in, a horse can be slowly introduced to the saddle. Instead of ambushing the horse with its first saddling, prepare the horse gradually in stages. Little things such as just getting the horse comfortable with the saddle pad or using a lead rope to simulate the cinch going around the horse's girth area can make a big difference when the real saddle arrives. And when the saddle is on, if the horse feels the need to run around a little, you make sure it runs in a safe

Above: Starting a Young Horse
Clinics have become popular as a way to get a young horse started under saddle. Arizona clinician Paul Dietz gets the horse used to the saddle blanket before he brings out the saddle. (Photo by Stephanie Levy)

Left: His New Saddle
This young horse is being started under saddle by his owner under the guidance of an experienced horseman at a clinic.

At a clinic, the young horses are often turned out into a big arena once saddled; this gives them a chance to turn their focus to the other horses instead of the saddle. (Photo by Gena McGrath)

93

Carrying the Weight

This colt has probably been saddled a couple times and allowed to run loose to become more comfortable with carrying the saddle. Clinician Paul Dietz gives the horse a taste of what it is like to have the weight of a human in the saddle. (Photo by Stephanie Levy)

pen where it is free to buck around a little until it understands that the saddle isn't that frightening or inhibiting.

Sometimes this new way of starting horses under saddle can seem the long way around to those who still subscribe to the old school. But as one master at this method puts it, sometimes the slowest way in the short run is the fastest in the long run, especially when you don't have to go back and fix problems later on. This method is less stressful for the horse than the old methods, where the horse might have struggled enough to break a leg or even its neck. It seems that by allowing the horse to move rather than restricting it when it responds to the saddle, the horse can remain more relaxed and ultimately lead a longer rideable life.

THE CALIFORNIOS

The fast-paced world has become faster paced in every respect, and the cowboy lifestyle is no exception. Enter a group called The Californios, a tribute to the traditional Spanish vaquero. This group uses a slower method to train a riding horse. In The Californios discipline, horses are taught to be responsive to the rider's slightest direction while tending to cattle out on the range, singling out a cow in the sorting pen, or bringing a calf to the branding fire.

The Californios style educates riding horses with a four-stage process, which differs from other training processes. Notably, with sparse feed and less advanced nutritional and veterinary support than today, the vaqueros of old started their horses under saddle much later than the current norm of two years old, giving the horse time to mature slowly before having to do the strenuous physical work required of a ranch horse.

Originally the vaqueros' horses were started in a bridle known as a "hackamore," which consists of reins and a bosal, a braided rawhide loop that encircles the horse's nose. Horses were usually three to four years old when started in the hackamore, an age when the horse's teeth are making final changes in maturity. The hackamore offered the horse more comfort than a metal bit in its mouth would.

Today, the process plays out in four stages. A horse's initial education is in a gentle bit called the "snaffle," which has a jointed mouthpiece and no leverage. The snaffle was introduced by the British during the colonial period. Modern "vaquero style" traditionalists start a horse in the snaffle bit, before moving on to the hackamore. Once a horse has progressed to a certain level of training in the hackamore, usually by age five or six, the horse is ready for the next stage, known as "the two-rein."

In the beginning of the two-rein stage, the rider changes to a smaller version of the hackamore called a "pencil bosal," or

The Californios

Following in the tradition of the vaqueros, Dave Weaver and his wife, Gwynn Turnbull Weaver, have organized an annual event, "The Californios," that showcases the old-style roping and cow work that once was the pride of the West. (Photo by Gwynn Turnbull Weaver)

Works of Art
During the final stage in the vaquero style of educating a horse, the spade bit is used. While it may look harsh, only the most educated of horses wear this bit. If the rider is experienced enough to get his horse to this stage, the rider's hands already know how to use this kind of bit. (Photo by Cheryl Kimball)

Branding
At the 2005 Californios event, two cowboys demonstrate how to rope and brand or doctor cattle. (Photo by Cheryl Kimball)

"two-rein bosal." This small bosal sits under a more traditional leather bridle and has its own small reins that lie parallel to the bridle reins. The classic spade bit is added to the horse's mouth so that it can simply become comfortable with the feel of such a bit in its mouth. Throughout the two-rein stage, the rider picks up on the reins of the spade bit more and more in preparation for the time when the "pencil bosal" will be removed.

Eventually the horse is ridden using just the spade bit with a small "bosalita," a tiny remnant of the hackamore, used only as a mark of distinction for the horse, which at this advanced stage of its education is referred to as "straight up in the bridle." The spade bit is a large iron bit, typically adorned with sterling silver inlay, consisting of a tall mouthpiece, or "port," and ornate iron cheek pieces that attached to the reins. The spade is known as a "signal bit." It is not used for leverage, but rather merely telegraphs the rider's minute hand movements to the horse's mouth. At the "straight up" stage, the horse is considered fully educated or "finished."

The mane of a horse trained in this manner is cut in specific patterns that indicate the horse's stage in the training process. This way, the cowboy can easily pick the appropriate horse out of the "cavvy" (the cowboy's group of horses to ride) for the job at hand. And if anyone else were to ride the horse, they would know the horse's level of education, ensuring that it will be ridden accordingly.

The Truth About Whispering
By the time novelist Nicholas Evans wrote *The Horse Whisperer* in 1995, I had been going to horse clinics—workshops where you learn about working with horses, from handling to riding, taught by an experienced horse person—for several years. The methods and approach taught in such clinics were brought to the general public via Evans' novel. To the best of my knowledge, this method was not referred to as "whispering" before the book was published; Evans either coined the phrase himself or discovered it during the course of his research and expanded upon it.

While Evans' book opened up a new world to those who had never run across the approach to educating a horse that Robert Redford depicted in the movie, it also gave those teaching horse clinics a marketing tool. Suddenly everyone became a "horse whisperer" and used the publicity garnered from the movie to promote themselves. Several clinicians claimed that Evans based his main character, Tom Booker, on them.

I have participated in dozens of clinics with my horses and sat on the fence and watched dozens more on the East Coast, the West Coast, and locations in between. My conclusion is that there are two kinds of horse clinicians: those who are interested in educating horses and people and make a living doing it, and those who are interested in money and fame and have chosen horse clinics as a vehicle to that end. I prefer to learn from the former type of teacher. That said, even the clinicians who are backed by marketing machines and whose main concern is making money have dramatically improved the lives of backyard horses.

For years backyard horse owners turned to the professional trainer, who would take their young horse for a specified period of time, typically ninety days, and hand it back ready to ride. Today, many horse owners are looking for more of an all-encompassing experience than that; they want to be involved in every aspect of their horse's life and education.

The proliferation of clinics, which really began to blossom in the early nineties, has allowed almost everyone in the United States, Canada, Europe, Australia, and beyond access to some of the best horsemen and horsewomen in the world. These clinics often focus on helping people gain more respectful behavior from their horses; they teach riders how mutual respect between a horse and rider leads to better behaved, safer horses. Riding is, of course, a focus of clinics, but without learning how to present yourself to a horse when you're on the ground, you probably won't be too successful in the saddle. In other words, if standing

beside your horse means it is using you as a scratching post or diving for grass and dragging you around as it eats or perhaps you never quite know if it is going to step on your foot, then you aren't going to get any more respect than that when you ride the horse. When you get on this horse's back, it will at worst run away with you or at least ignore you, treating you as if you are as bothersome as a gnat.

Whatever the professional horse trainer's education skills, the horse will always operate at the level of its rider—the more experienced equestrian can get a lot more response out of the same horse that

Horse Clinics

Horse clinics have become a popular way for a group of people to learn about their horses' behavior from an experienced horseman. Once riders understand horse behavior they can get it working in their favor, making handling and riding more pleasant. (Photo by Cheryl Kimball)

Bucking Bronco

A person starting a young horse under saddle would like to know about and hopefully desensitize these touchy spots before climbing on. This rope around the horse's girth area simulates a tightened back girth and can help the horse understand that these things aren't a threat to the horse's life; perhaps by the time the saddle is strapped on he won't feel so defensive about it. (Photo by Rick Larsen)

is giving a less experienced rider trouble. This principle plays out when owners get their horses home from the trainer. If the rider lacks experience, confidence, or especially consistency, the horse gradually drifts backward in its education. The horse won't do what the rider thinks she or he is requesting, rider/owner becomes afraid of the horse, and often the horse goes back to the trainer's for a tune-up. Trainers can find a certain amount of job security in this repeat business, which is great as long as no one, including the horse, gets hurt in the process.

In the best-case clinic scenario, owners can take their horses to a clinic and spend three to five days learning from a top hand. Professional horse trainers who thought they'd lose business to the

clinics once viewed with skepticism these sessions where owners learned horsemanship skills they once turned to professionals for. But the savvy professional trainers have identified where their services might be of help. Smart horse professionals also attend the clinics in their area to learn the methods the clinician is teaching. Then clinic attendees can hire one of these professionals to help them follow through with what they have started to learn.

The clinics themselves have become a mildly booming industry for many small towns, bringing dozens of riders to stay in local hotels, eat in local restaurants, and buy things at the local convenience store.

Riding Behaviors

Being ridden is not something that comes naturally to a horse. Having another living thing climb onto its back and hang on must remind the horse of a predator, giving it a reason to buck and run. The fact that horses can learn to tolerate a human rider is practically a miracle. There are some undesirable riding behaviors that we can instill in horses, however, without even realizing it.

HERD-BOUNDNESS

Domestic horses spend the majority of their time with their barn mates and a relatively small amount of time with their human pals. No wonder when we saddle up and head out on the trail, many horses are reluctant to leave their companions. This reluctance—exhibited in many different ways from just refusing to move to bucking or running back to the barn—is referred to as "barn sour" or "herd bound." It takes a fair amount of good horsemanship for a horse to be so comfortable with its rider that it will enjoy being with the rider as much as with its equine friends.

Some horses care less than others about going away from the herd, and this so-called herd-boundness is never an issue. Some learn to not care, feeling confident that they will return to the herd in short order. Some do not exhibit herd-boundness with some riders but are less confident with other riders. Some care a lot and try every trick up their sleeves—bucking, rearing, galloping back uncontrollably to the barn entrance, or, worse yet, into the barn itself no matter how low the doorway—to convince their riders that putting them back in the stall or corral is the best idea. The horse seems to just want to be back at the barn, where things are familiar, predictable, and not very taxing.

Some horses seem to get bored and look forward to a little time away from the barn. These horses actually welcome the change in environment and enjoy going out on a trail ride. This can be especially true of performance horses, which often spend a lot of time training and competing in a riding ring. For some performance horses, going out on the trail can be scary compared to the relative safety of riding around a ring, but to others, getting out on the trail regularly can make them happier with their ring work. If you work in an office all week and look forward to some rock climbing or sailing (or horseback riding) on the weekends, you know how many performance horses feel about trail rides.

BUCKING

Bucking is perhaps the negative horse behavior with which people, of the horsey set or not, are most familiar. Rodeos make a sport out of it, and events allow riders to show off their ability to ride a bucking horse. To a horse, bucking is a built-in defense mechanism used to get a predator off its back.

When a horse is learning to carry a saddle and rider, it may well buck when it first moves with a saddle tightened to its back. Some may buck the first time a rider puts additional weight on its back and wraps his or her legs around the horse's sides, making the horse feel confined. A rider who is experienced at starting young colts under saddle will know that pulling on both reins or gripping with his or her legs can make a young horse inexperienced with being ridden feel too confined. And if the horse starts to buck, the experienced rider will know how to

The horse that has checked out and learned not to listen to a rider's inconsistent messages is said to be "dull." People often mistake a dull horse for a horse that is kind and has come to like and trust people enough to be gentle. But gentle and dull are not the same thing. If a dull horse comes out of its coma, it can be a frustrating and dangerous thing for the rider—instead of tuning everything out, the horse tunes everything in and reacts to it.

ride through it and be able to stop the bucking as soon as possible.

Just how a horse will behave under saddle often depends on how well the horse was prepared to accept something on its back. The personality of the horse is also a factor. Some horses never buck in their entire lifetime, while others seem to take off bucking for no apparent reason.

When a saddle horse carries this bucking tendency into adulthood, after it has experience being ridden, something probably went wrong in the horse's early riding experience. A trainer may be able to cure bucking tendencies by going back and working through some of the foundation stages of saddling and riding; other times the tendency is with the horse for life. That's a good reason to stay away from the horse named Bucky or Bronc when you go for one of those pay-by-the-hour trail rides!

REARING

Rearing refers to when a horse stands up on its hind legs. It is another defense mechanism similar to bucking, used when the horse feels the need to get something (like a rider) off its back, to appear larger to a predator, or to strike most effectively with its front legs. As athletic as they are, horses have a hard time balancing all that weight up in the air. When a horse rears, there is the danger of it standing up so straight that it offsets its center of gravity

and tips over backward, threatening to land on the rider.

Horses rear not only when afraid, but also when they feel they can't move, such as when beginning riders encourage the horse to move forward by bumping its sides with their legs, but then they become afraid of it moving too fast and pull back on the reins, signaling to the horse slow down or stop. So they are telling the horse to move and stop at the same time—confusing at best! If a horse is allowed complete freedom of movement, bucking and rearing can be reduced, if not eliminated. The goal, of course, is to teach the horse that when you are on its back or leading it, its movements are at your direction. But you must be consistent in how you ask for the horse to move or you will confuse it. And surely no one wants to be astride a confused half-ton animal.

In Your Favor

The key to having a lovely relationship with a horse is to get the instincts that can cause all of these potential negative behaviors working in your favor for positive results. I have been frustrated with my horses over the years, sometimes feeling as if I have caused certain behaviors, especially those related to riding. But once I began to better understand good horsemanship and worked toward applying it, I have found horse behavior, whether I caused it or not, more fascinating than frustrating.

One turning point in my own horsemanship education came at a big horsemanship demonstration I attended a few years ago. Ray Hunt, a top horseman in the world today, was riding a mare, and a large group of other highly skilled horsemen and horsewomen were riding with him. They all left the arena and, as emcee of the event, Ray stayed behind on his mare to talk to the audience. His mare desperately wanted to leave with the other horses. She began prancing around and, if he had given her the opportunity, she would have bolted through the gate to catch up.

Ray worked with the mare to get her to be more interested in what he wanted to be doing, rather than in having to be with those other horses. He explained that in his opinion the mare was entitled to her own thoughts about the situation. His responsibility as her rider was to replace those thoughts with his thoughts—to let his idea of staying behind become her idea too. Over the course of twenty minutes, while he talked with the audience, Ray trotted the mare in circles, figure eights, and generally showed her that if she was prancing and fired up about bolting off with her friends, she would have to stay behind longer and do some work. Once she calmed down and could stand quietly, he let her leave. Ray Hunt has often said, "Someone has to be in charge of this outfit, so it might as well be you." I like to keep this in mind when I ride. While the best riders allow the horse to make some decisions (riders should certainly consider taking a different route when a horse refuses to go over what may be an unsafe bridge!), ultimately for the safety of you both, the rider's decisions should go unquestioned.

Rearing Horse

Rearing is used to strike at predators or to attempt to get something—a predator, a saddle, or a rider—off its back. A horse may also rear if it is getting mixed messages from a rider or handler about whether to go backward or forward. (Photo © Alan & Sandy Carey)

101

Chapter Five

In the Ring, On the Track, and Along the Trail:

The Competitive Horse

Charlie Hood Leaving "Conclusion" © R. R. Doubleda

According to the American Horse Council, the 6.9 million horses in the United States today are owned by 1.9 million people. Of these, 725,000 horses are used for racing. 1,974,000 are used for showing. And 2,970,000 are kept for recreational purposes. Another 1,262,800 are used for other purposes such as ranching, rodeo, polo, mounted police work, and farming.

Sidesaddle Jumping
Jumping a horse can be intimidating enough but some make it that much more challenging by doing it sidesaddle! (Photo by Laura Cotterman)

The Rodeo Circuit
Rodeos have been around as long as the cowboys themselves. Started by cowboys as a form of entertainment on their day off and a chance to show their prowess with horses and bulls, rodeos are now big-money events and full-time work for "cowboys," many of whom have never worked on a ranch.

A sk any rider who has been out on the trail attempting a nice slow canter alongside a riding companion, and they'll tell you that most horses have a natural competitive streak. That nice canter can quickly turn into a hell-bent-for-leather gallop, with one horse desperate to get ahead of the other and the finish line a mystery to all. Horse owners know that the horses racing in a herd around the track at Churchill Downs are happy to be there for the most part.

Since it seems so natural for horses to enjoy competition, it also seems natural for horseowners to involve their horses in competitive sports. From the mega-complex world of professional horseracing to a bunch of friends spending a Friday evening trying to maneuver a few cows into a pen before the buzzer goes off, competing with

Rodeo cowboys seem to literally graduate from the school of hard knocks! They wear back braces and other protective gear, but mostly learn how to move in rhythm with the horse's movements to keep themselves from getting too hurt—and staying on board the eight seconds required to post a score. (Shutterstock Photo)

The Bucking Horse

Rodeo bucking horses are not really competing against the rider; they are just interested in dumping an annoyance off their backs. While most young horses started under saddle are encouraged to ride out smoothly and feel comfortable with a saddle and rider, the horse headed for the bucking chute is encouraged to do just the opposite. If there's something clinging to its back, the bucking horse is trained to shed it at all costs.

Typically the bucking horse has a strap cinched up into its tender flank area. The cinch doesn't have to be tight enough to hurt the horse; horses that have not been desensitized to this back cinch will often buck when it is tightened up just enough to secure it. But "good" bucking horses don't often need a bucking strap to set them off.

Although a hard-bucking horse looks like it is having a miserable time, the good ones actually lead a pretty nice life. They are expected to buck hard for less than eight seconds at a turn, and they are generally extremely well fed and cared for, because there is no value in a bucking horse that is too sick or weak to buck.

horses is a common pursuit. Horseback riders have even managed to turn trail riding into a judged competitive sport, and long-distance "endurance" trail riding is becoming increasingly popular.

Each activity requires its own gear. Long distance riders use lots of the same equipment that runners and hikers use, such as water "camels" (water-filled backpacks filled with a long straw that curls around to the rider's mouth), fanny packs for emergency first-aid items and snake bite kits, and heart-rate and respiration monitors for the horse. Polo players need mallets, balls, and wraps for their horses' legs. Serious competitors in the cutting horse world often spend several thousand dollars on a mechanical cow with which to practice.

Racing

Although the Kentucky Derby, the Preakness Stakes, and the Belmont Stakes are steeped in tradition, they are young events in horseracing's overall history. Horse racing has been around since humans first got cozy with horses. Like many sports that have evolved from more practical purposes, chariot racing and jousting were equine sporting activities that emanated from the skills required to use horses in battle.

The Romans were chariot-racing aficionados. In their eyes, the more bloody and violent the event the better. The

Equi-speak

The phrase to "get your goat"—as in, "Don't believe Dad about the monster under the bed, he's just trying to get your goat"—originated in the horseracing world. During their racing careers, racehorses spend a lot of time alone in a stall. They are confined mainly to prevent them from using up their energy cavorting around a pasture with other horses, but also so they don't get injured in the process. Racehorses also regularly travel to different tracks, where they are stall bound.

Horses are social animals, so this time alone can be tough on some. Enter the goat. Neutered male goats, called "wethers," became the companions of choice for many racehorses. Horses typically become so attached to their goat mate that the goat travels with them on the road to distant racetracks, helping to keep their charge content and calm. Racing legend has it that if you wanted to get your rival's horse all steamed up and out of sorts before a big race, you would steal the horse's companion—or go "get its goat."

Romans built the Circus Maximus in Rome around the sixth century B.C., and the structure accommodated a quarter million spectators—an enthusiastic crowd that makes current ballgame brawls seem like spats in a playground sandbox. The track was conveniently set up to ensure a spectacular convergence of wildly excited horses at the first turn. The winner was a minor point, prearranged for sure with corruption a given. Although the winning

Cooling Down

Horses cannot be simply put in their stall while hot from a workout or competition. Cooling down a horse is an art in itself. Lightweight blankets made of cotton mesh, fleece, or wool can help speed up the process. But the best way to cool down a horse is to simply walk him around until his heart and respiration rates are back to normal and his body no longer feels hot to the touch. (Shutterstock Photo)

team was announced by the umpire, no one watching could tell, nor cared, who actually finished the race and in what order. Emperors Caligula and Nero were fans of the races.

Today, we know racing—at least on the surface, if not behind the scenes—as a much more civilized undertaking, the "sport of kings" or commonly called the "blood sport" (as in "blue blood"). Gambling has helped move horse racing to the seedy side of town, to be sure. But to the casual observer who neither rides nor bets, horse racing is the fanciful sport

THE KENTUCKY DERBY · CHURCHILL DOWNS
128TH RUNNING · MAY 4, 2002

Mint Juleps, the Hat Parade, and Celebrity Watching: The Nonhorse Side of the Kentucky Derby

Much of what has become tradition at the Kentucky Derby has little do to with horses. After all, the race itself is dubbed "the greatest two minutes in sports" because, well, it lasts less than two minutes. But the rules of hype dictate that a two-minute event be stretched into a week-long extravaganza, so other attractions have been added over the years to make for an exciting time at the track. Attractive and often famous women in gaudy hats sipping mint juleps are perhaps as synonymous with the Derby as the thundering hooves. We can't all be famous, of course, but mint juleps—ah, there is something in which we can all partake on an early summer afternoon right in our own backyards.

The KENTUCKY DERBY

CHURCHILL DOWNS
129TH RUNNING
MAY 3RD 2003

The horses are not the only things on display at the Kentucky Derby. The style conscious come out for the festivities dressed in their finest hats and dresses and suits. (Used Courtesy of Claire Jett)

The Kentucky Derby has been run since 1875 and is nicknamed the "run for the roses" because the winning horse is draped with a blanket of red roses. (Used Courtesy of Claire Jett)

Horse sense is the thing a horse has which keeps it from betting on people.
–W.C. Fields

DERBY DAY

Derby Day

The Kentucky Derby is always run the first Sunday in the month of May at Churchill Downs racetrack in Louisville, Kentucky. (Used Courtesy of Claire Jett)

seen on network television three times a year in the spring, when the Kentucky Derby, the Preakness, and the Belmont Stakes, known collectively as the famous Triple Crown, are run. As of this writing, no horse has won all three since 1978, when the teenaged jockey Stephen Cauthen rode the impressive horse Affirmed to triple victory.

Other types of popular horse racing include steeplechases and harness racing.

In a steeplechase, dozens of horses and riders race across a grass track, hurling themselves over thirty fences along a four-mile course. Many horse and rider teams never make it to the finish line. Although there are pockets of steeplechasing in the United States, the sport is firmly entrenched in British equine history. The first formal steeplechase was run at St. Albans in Great Britain in 1830. Just a few years later, the Grand National

Run, Run, Run

Sulky Race

Riders race their sulkies around the track at the Minnesota State Fair grounds, circa 1950 (Photo used courtesy of the Minnesota Historical Society).

Horse competition hasn't always been as organized as what we see at the racetrack today. Figure, the founding stud of the Morgan breed, was so small that everyone laughed when his owner suggested that the horse could pull a stubborn log out of the mud, a log that had frustrated several horses already. Figure was successful, but every drunken tavern customer still thought his horse could outrun the mighty little horse, and Figure and his owner, Justin Morgan, were challenged for many a race. Figure proved himself time and again to be the strongest and perhaps most competitive of them all.

The Mongolians have revered the horse for centuries. During the Nadaam festival each July, they race on open grassland. Children ages five through thirteen act as jockeys because of their light weight. As many as a thousand horses, divided into six categories according to age, race across the open range. The winning horses are rewarded by having songs and poems written about them.

Equi-celebrity Actor Julia Roberts lived with the Mongolians for a few weeks in the late nineties. The PBS television series Nature produced a fascinating account of the Mongolians and their relationship with their horses called "The Wild Horses of Mongolia with Julia Roberts", which aired in October 2000.

In the Homestretch

If these horses were at the finish line, the one on the "inside" next to the rail would be ahead by just about a "length," or the length of one horse/stride. This makes for an exciting finish, although "by a nose" is even more exciting, and a "photo finish" where only a still shot of the finish line can determine the winner, is the most exciting finish of all. (Shutterstock Photo)

took its place and is now as famous as the U.S.'s Kentucky Derby. Only one horse, Red Rum, has won the Grand National three times.

Harness racing is a tad less wild than steeplechasing. Harness racing is extremely popular in the United States but enjoys a following the world over. The horse of choice for harness racing is the Standardbred, which typically races in a gait called the "pace." In the

pace, the lateral legs of the horse—that is, both front and back legs on the same side—move simultaneously. (In a trot, by contrast, the front leg and its opposite hind leg move together.) No galloping is allowed in harness racing; if a horse breaks from the pace to a gallop, it is disqualified. Horses are often fitted with harnesses that hobble their legs so they can't easily break stride. The rider sits behind the horse in a two-wheeled cart

known as a sulky, careening around the track at speeds of around forty miles per hour. In thoroughbred racing under saddle, the horses are all led into separate compartments in the starting gate, which is a fairly permanent structure at the beginning of the racetrack. In order to accommodate the size of the sulkies, the harness racing starting gate does not have compartments and is attached to the back of a vehicle. The vehicle speeds out of the way and the starting gate folds in half as the race begins. And yes, there is big-time betting in harness racing.

Carreras de Caballos

Horse racing is popular in many countries of the world. Racetracks can either be dirt tracks or grass tracks, often consisting of mainly Bermuda grass. Horses race on both but some prove themselves better "grass horses" than others.

Starting the Merry Hunting
A painting by German artist Rudolf Schramm-Zittau illustrates the traditional fox hunt in Europe.

Fox Hunting

Another horse activity that evolved first out of practicality and then was perpetuated in the leisure time of the elite is fox hunting. There are active hunt clubs in almost every state in the United States. Whereas Kentucky is practically synonymous with horse racing, Virginia is the fox-hunting capital of the nation and home to the Masters of the Foxhounds Association of America.

Fox hunting is often thought of as closely tied to the United Kingdom, a belief that is perhaps perpetuated by media photos of Prince Charles and his sons cavorting through the fields in their hunt garb. England came under fire for

continuing to use live foxes, which are hunted to the death, a practice that was abandoned in the United States several years ago. Because rabies is nonexistent in England (as is true in most island nations, where highly communicable diseases are easier to control), the fox population is quite large, and residents want it controlled. Despite its British roots, fox hunting has a long history throughout the world, including in those nations once colonized by the British, such as India, as well as other countries, such as France.

Most equine activities have their rules and etiquette, but none are as strictly regulated in both behavior and attire as

Trail Riding

One of the most popular activities of recreational horseback riders is trail riding, sauntering through the countryside either with a couple of buddies or as an organized group. Preservation of open space for horseback riding is a common concern throughout the country but if you have a horse trailer and are a bit mobile, you can ride in many national parks, on beaches during the off season, and in many state and local forests. As this photo shows, fall can be the most stunning time for horseback riders to be out on the trail—the temperature and footing are usually perfect, the bugs are at bay, and the scenery is fantastic. (Photo by Laura Cotterman)

fox hunting. Hunt clubs are highly organized groups. Individual hunt members and riders own their horses, but hounds are typically owned by the club. The hunt includes some key participants, whose roles are well defined:

The Master of the Hounds has the overall command of the hunt, both in the field and around the kennels. This high-profile position requires some good schmoozing skills to encourage landowners to allow the club to use their private land (a huge issue in many equine activities), since good fox hunts cover a lot of ground and clubs like to vary where they hunt.

The Huntsman is responsible for the hounds in the field.

Whippers-in assist the huntsman, helping control the hounds and scout the fox.

The Field Master is in charge of controlling the field, or group of riders.

The Secretary is the details person, tending to such things as reports of damaged fences.

It can be quite intimidating to be a beginner riding with a hunt club (read Michael Korda's book *Horse People* for some hilarious descriptions of fox hunting), but clubs are often looking for new members, and there is a well-orchestrated effort to help newcomers understand the rules of the hunt.

Polo Match at Fort Snelling
The Fort Snelling Blacks battled against the Twin Cities team in this circa 1931 polo match played on the grounds of the fort. (Photo used courtesy of the Minnesota Historical Society)

Polo

Polo is a horse activity so old that no one knows exactly when it was first actually played. It is thought to have originated in China and Persia around 2000 years ago. The first recorded polo game was played in 600 B.C. between the Turkomans and the Persians. The Ottoman Turks, according to legend, used human heads as polo balls. In ancient times there could be as many as fifty players on the field, but the current standard of play involves four players on each team.

Polo has long been considered a sport for the wealthy and with good reason. To play this vigorous game—which is done mostly at a full gallop—one needs to have several horses, known as a "string of polo ponies." There are eight, seven-and-a-half-minute periods, or "chukkers," in a standard polo game, and horses are switched at every chukker. Most horses are rotated back into the game after a few chukkers' rest, unless they were injured. (The horses' legs are well wrapped to prevent injury but in such a high-paced activity injuries are inevitable.)

Polo ponies in the hands of good riders seem to have a lot of fun playing the game. Like horses that work with cattle, polo ponies are required to be agile and move freely and precisely. Those best suited for the game are thought to actually follow the ball as a horse does a cow.

A sister sport to polo is polocrosse, a game that is in some ways simpler than polo. Polocrosse has also been around for hundreds of years. Players use a racket similar to the one used in lacrosse to scoop up the ball. Teams consist of six players with three on the field at a time, alternating between chukkers. Polocrosse also has a smaller arena requirement—60 by 160 feet, similar in size to many indoor riding arenas. But the biggest difference between polocrosse and polo is that polocrosse players must ride one horse for the whole game.

Horse Showing

Of all the competitive opportunities for horses, the one that the backyard, one- or two-horse owner tends to get into most often is horse showing. Horse showing accounts for almost one-third of the 40 billion dollars reportedly spent in the U.S. horse industry each year. Showing horses can be as simple as heading to your local show club's ring with Old Dusty one afternoon to walk, trot, and canter around with a couple of your riding pals. Or it can be as complex as showing in an upper-level "circuit," where competitors travel every weekend to attend horse shows in distant cities, riding in the ring with dozens of other competitors. Both ends of the horse-showing spectrum seem to be alive and well.

Here Comes the Judge

At a horse show, the judge rules. The judge's decision is final and often can be challenged only through a formal process, if at all. Show etiquette and good sportsmanship does not allow competitors to speak directly to the judge when they are in the ring competing; to speak with the judge usually requires getting permission from the ring steward or some other official.

Good Jump

Riders performing in stadium jumping must follow a prescribed course around several jumps set up in an arena. The events are typically timed and "faults" whenever rails are knocked off the jumps. (Shutterstock Photo)

Showing In Hand

Showing a horse "in hand" is common in several classes in horse shows. Halter classes typically require the horses to simply stand in a line where they are judged against each other based on physical characteristics. Other in-hand classes may require the handler to walk and trot the horse through a pattern. (Photo by Laura Cotterman)

Even within the horse show world, there is a wide range of types of shows and of classes within shows. For instance, my local club, which has been around for more than thirty years, hosts pleasure shows, gymkhanas (focusing on games on horseback), and shows specifically for miniature horses.

Riders get into horse showing because it gives them a specific goal for their horse, their riding, and their horsemanship. Unless you get into the upper echelon of showing, the only expenses to show your horse include class entry fees, stall fees, overnight accommodations, and gas. The upper ranks of shows and competitions (such as those focused on jumping or on cattle work) offer reasonable but elusive

purses. Typically, horse shows that offer a purse are those with a lot of action, meaning there is the potential for riders to fall or get bucked off. Action draws spectators, which in turn helps attract sponsors.

PICK A SHOW, ANY SHOW

There are many different kinds of horse shows. Some incorporate jumping classes or trail classes into their general show, while others focus exclusively on jumping. The American Quarter Horse Association (AQHA) has started a "ranch versatility show," which involves five different events, including cutting cows and other ranch-type work, a "pleasure" class (where riders just go around in a circle and generally show off how comfortable their horse is to ride), and a halter class with equipment and attire expectations in line with the ranch focus (i.e., working equipment not lots of sparkling silver).

Other shows are breed specific. Shows can also be classed by level of rider, from amateur to professional, and some shows feature different classes for each level.

A couple of more locally based horse shows that the everyday backyard rider might encounter include gymkhanas and pleasure-horse shows.

Gymkhanas are action-packed horse shows consisting of different games, such as barrel racing (running fast around barrels), pole bending (running fast around poles), and table top. Table top is a game where participants ride as fast as they can from the starting line to a table, jump off their horse, walk around the table top, climb back on their horse, and ride as fast as they can back to the start line; often the rider's biggest challenge is to hang onto the horse while they are on the table. Other games such as "egg-and-spoon" and "fanny" rides require competitors to ride smoothly enough to hold an egg in a spoon or a dollar bill under their butt. Gymkhanas attract many young riders.

So-called pleasure-horse shows have various classes designed to show how pleasant your horse is to ride and how nicely you ride it. Typically, the class participants ride around the ring in both directions at a walk, trot, and canter. When they get to the center-of-the-ring lineup, participants show how well their horses back up. Judges expect horses to be easygoing, to hold their head up and ears forward, to change gaits when asked, and to behave well around other horses.

Equitation classes judge the rider instead of the horse. Riders should be able to give their horses subtle cues, have quiet legs and arms, post or sit the trot, ride the canter without flopping around in the saddle, and be smartly appointed (both horse and rider) for their chosen discipline. For the upper-level shows, riders might even consult color coaches who help them choose outfits where the

pieces not only coordinate but also best match their horse's color.

THE ALL-AMERICAN QUARTER HORSE CONGRESS

Each October, the Ohio Quarter Horse Association in Columbus hosts the annual All-American Quarter Horse Congress, an absolutely enormous horse show drawing almost ten thousand Quarter Horses and thousands of owners each year. The show horses are divided into classes, which consist of everything from in-hand classes where horses are shown in just a halter to pleasure riding in English and Western saddles, jumping, and reining. (In reining, riders follow a pattern that involves riding fast, sliding to a stop, riding in tight circles, then wide circles, and other complex moves.) Many classes at the Congress have hundreds of riders, making it necessary for riders to come

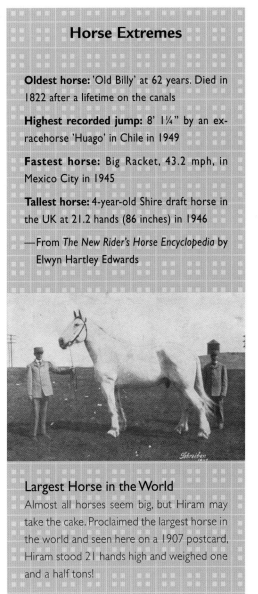

Largest Horse in the World
Almost all horses seem big, but Hiram may take the cake. Proclaimed the largest horse in the world and seen here on a 1907 postcard, Hiram stood 21 hands high and weighed one and a half tons!

Pole Bending
Pole bending is an event at games shows (known as "gymkhanas") and rodeos, where horse and rider run around a set of poles. These events are timed and speed is of utmost importance. (Shutterstock Photos)

117

Cross Country
The cross country course of a three-phase event (the other two phases being dressage and stadium jumping, both performed in the arena setting) is not for the meek of heart. Jumps are high and wide and many involve hills and water. (Shutterstock Photo)

ers compete for the world championship title in eighty-six different classes, including jumping, trail, reining, and pleasure riding. Many make American Quarter Horse showing a family affair, as this event provides opportunities for young riders to showcase their talents.

The Olympics

Olympic equestrian events are one of the few places in upper-level competitive sports where women and men compete on equal footing. The current three Olympic equestrian events are dressage, show jumping (jumping in a stadium), and three-day eventing, which combines the latter two with cross country, where riders jump along a more natural course outdoors.

For several years, equestrians have been petitioning the International Olympic Committee for a Western-riding Olympic event. So far, reining seems to have the best potential for being added as the next new equestrian event. Endurance riding, not specifically a Western pursuit, is also under consideration. The decision is not yet final, so don't expect to see either of these events too soon. The good news is that media coverage of equestrian Olympics has been stepped up over the past few years to satisfy a growing desire among horse lovers to b e able to see these events.

New ways to compete with your horse are cropping up all the time. Jousting

into the ring in batches. The Congress lasts almost three weeks, and the winners of the early classes compete in final classes late in the show.

If the classes at the American Quarter Horse Congress aren't enough to keep spectators busy, there are hundreds of retail exhibits selling everything from the 350-dollar sparkling sequined blouses to horse figurines. The Congress also offers equine lectures and demonstrations.

Proving how popular the American Quarter Horse is and how well the AQHA promotes the breed, qualifying horses and riders travel from Columbus to Oklahoma City less than a month later for a huge, two-week long AQHA World Show. Showing for the year culminates here, where hardworking horses and rid-

Jousting

Jousting has become a popular horse activity and is even the state sport of Maryland! (Shutterstock Photo)

The Tevis Cup

Marathon runners must pay close attention to things like hydration, energy level, and heart rate. Endurance trail riders must do the same—for themselves and for their horses.

Endurance horseback riding consists of trail rides of between twenty-five and fifty miles per day. The Tevis Cup, technically known as the Western States Trail Ride, is considered the ultimate equine endurance challenge. It takes place every August in Northern California's Sierra Nevada region. With a motto of "to finish is to win," the Tevis Cup ride traverses 100 miles in twenty-four hours, starting near Lake Tahoe and crossing through the Sierra Nevada—a tough 100 miles by any measure.

The annual ride began in 1955, at a time when the era of horse-as-transportation was coming to a close and when modern-day horses were thought to be unable to endure the kind of riding their predecessors had. Will Tevis, a prominent businessman in San Francisco in the mid-twentieth century, provided financial support in the early days of the ride and named the event in honor of his grandfather, Lloyd Tevis. Riders must make their horse's condition the priority, keeping close tabs on the horse throughout the ride. Arabian and Arabian crosses, known for their stamina and high energy level, are often the breed of choice in endurance riding. The horse that wins the Western States Trail Ride is deemed "fit to continue"—in other words, by the end of the ride the horse isn't completely spent.

(the state sport of Maryland), cowboy-mounted shooting, and so-called Natural Horsemanship-type competitions are just a few events that have entered the competitive horse world. Some competitions are expensive to follow, others not so much. But whatever the rider chooses to do, what's most important is to enjoy the sport and try to help the horse enjoy it, too.

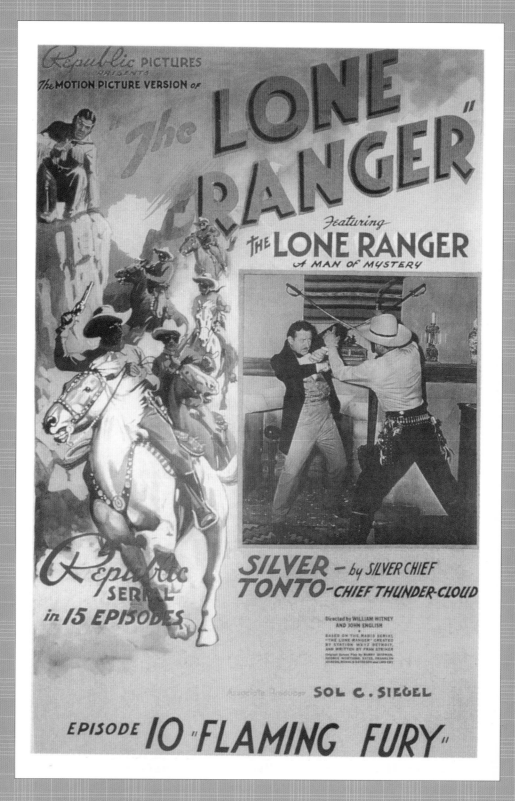

Famous Equines:
The Horse in Popular Culture

Left: The Lone Ranger

The Lone Ranger and his horse Silver first joined forces with Tonto and his horse Scout in the fight against evil beginning in 1933 on WXYZ radio in Detroit. In 1938, the duo hit the big screen in a fifteen-chapter serial, followed in 1939 by a second serial in fifteen parts, *The Lone Ranger Rides Again*. It became a television show in 1949, when Clayton Moore first donned the black mask.

Roping Cowboy

A smiling cowboy ropes in readers of *Roy Rogers* Comics, encouraging them to read about a special offer.

Horses are not just for horse lovers. It is clear that horses have become part of our popular culture in a big way. They are in the movies, on the television screen, and at one time, they were even on the radio. Horses and horse-related motifs have been used to decorate everything from dinner plates to silk scarves. Images of horses prance across pajamas and sheets. Hobby horses (stuffed toy horse heads on sticks) are a favorite toy that kids love to "ride" around. Despite the diminished role that real horses play in contemporary society, they are clearly a permanent part of our popular culture.

Ferrari's Famous Horse

Symbols of horses inspired automakers ever since the horseless carriage was first invented to displace steeds. From Ford's Mustang to the stallion in Porsche's shield logo, the most famous remains Ferrari's *cavallino rampante*, or prancing horse, insignia that graces the Italian racing and sports cars. Enzo Ferrari adopted the insignia from an Italian fighter ace of World War I; he placed it on a yellow field, the official color of his own hometown of Modena. (Photo © Michael Dregni)

Collectibles

At one point or another, anything and everything seems to have been adorned by a horse or equestrian-related image. Some of these collectibles are used in horse activities, while others just sport an equine motif.

Collecting horse paraphernalia is popular enough that people like Fredricka Olson of New Hampshire made a business out of buying and selling all things horse. Freddi's father served in the 101st Cavalry in World War II, spurring her own lifelong interest in horses. Freddi started collecting equine antiques and collectibles many years ago, decided to

Model Shows

Nearly every young girl, whether she has a real horse in the barn or not, loves ceramic and plastic horse models. Breyer plastic models dominate the market. When Breyer made a horse model to adorn a clock in 1950, the model itself was so popular that the company decided to give up clock production and focus entirely on the horse models. Today, the models are still hand painted, and each one is somewhat distinctive.

These days Breyer's astute marketing techniques hold the interest of its collectors. The company produces a collector's magazine, *Just About Horses*, and releases new models regularly that reflect the horse flavor of the month, such

Breyer Model

This model of Dreamer was created in conjunction with the release of the 2005 movie of the same name. (Photo by Cheryl Kimball)

as a Triple Crown contender or main equine character of a movie such as *The Horse Whisperer, Seabiscuit,* or *Dreamer*. Most breeds are well represented, and there are stables and riding equipment with which to outfit the models. Breyer even sponsors model "horse shows" around the country, as well as an annual "Breyerfest!" that takes place each July at the Kentucky Horse Park in Lexington.

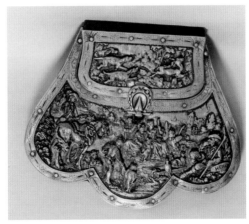

Equestrian by Design

Horses have been used in the decoration of just about everything from plates (top left) to purses (top middle). Items such as stirrup cups (top right) used to toast a good ride at the end of a fox hunt have become collector's items. And items designed to be used in the barn such as this saddle rack (bottom left) and whip holder (bottom right) have been incorporated into household décor and re-purposed as utensil holders, coat racks, and myriad other things. (Photos courtesy of Freddi Olson)

make a business out of her passion, and now has sold items to collectors all over the world. People who have never even seen a live horse use antique tack-room furnishings and other equestrian items to furnish entire rooms in horse themes, using bits as curtain tiebacks and stall grilles to hang pots and pans. Many items that no longer have as big a place in the contemporary horse world, such as brass harness medallions and bridle rosettes, have become fodder for the collectibles market. Until she moved her original shop a couple of years ago and sold off the large pieces, Freddi even had a number of antique buggies for sale. Her offering includes old books on horse and animal husbandry, empty containers of horse liniments and other medicines, as well as old horse shoes and even tea sets designed for picnics via horseback or horse-drawn cart—Freddi's collection is great fun for the equestrian and nonrider alike.

The Horse in Art

The horse captivated Leonardo da Vinci, just more proof of the power the equine form holds over humans. And da Vinci was far from alone in the artist-as-horse-lover capacity. Painters, sculptors, and

Da Vinci's Horse

Da Vinci's American horse statue is located in the Frederic Meijer Gardens in Grand Rapids. This aerial view gives viewers a sense of the enormity of the statue. (Photo by William J. Hebert Photography, courtesy Frederik Meijer Gardens and Sculpture Park)

Les Cheveaux de Courses

This painting, by French impressionist Edgar Degas (1834–1917), is one of many he created during the 1870s that featured jockeys on horseback. (© Christie's Images/SuperStock)

illustrators have taken on the horse in one way or another since nearly the beginning of time.

LEONARDO DA VINCI'S HORSE

American Charles Dent read an article in *National Geographic* in 1977 that sent the retired Pennsylvania airline pilot on a life's mission. In that article, Dent learned that Leonardo da Vinci, the Renaissance man of all Renaissance men, had been commissioned by the Duke of Sforza to create the largest equine statue ever.

Leonardo da Vinci never got around to creating the bronze statue that he designed. He did, however, create a twenty-four-foot clay model, which was destroyed by French archers who used it for practice. Notebooks of working sketches, which had been lost, reappeared in 1966. Charles Dent took it on himself to see that the statue was created—one in

Italy, of course, as was originally intended, and one for America as well—reportedly as a gesture of thanks for all that the Renaissance has meant to American and world culture. Although Dent had a great talent for fundraising and was able to pull together not only financial support but also artists and other workers needed for the project, it was his own money, left in his will, that funded the project after his death in 1994.

The cast for the statue was made at the Tallix Art Foundry in Beacon, New York, and the final sculpting of the master model was done by Nina Akamu, along with a team of seven other people. The final horses weighed in at fifteen tons. The American statue is located in the Frederick Meijer Gardens in Grand Rapids, Michigan. The Italian statue was flown courtesy of Alitalia to Milan, where it resides in the San Siro Hippodrome.

GEORGE STUBBS

George Stubbs (1724–1806) was a self-taught British painter. His favorite subjects were animals in general and horses in particular. Stubbs launched a successful career as an equine portrait artist in 1766 with the publication of his *Anatomy of the Horse*, which remains a greatly admired work. Stubbs' many horse paintings include *Racehorses Belonging to the Duke of Richmond Exercising at Goodwood, Horse Attacked by a Lion, Mares and Foals Disturbed by an Approaching Storm,* and many others.

EDWEARD MUYBRIDGE

The eccentric Edward Muybridge was known for many things, but he was perhaps most famous for his serial photography of the trotting horse. Muybridge took the photos in June 1878 to successfully prove Leland Stanford's claim that for a split second during a horse's running stride all four feet leave the ground. The

Pumpkin with a Stable Lad

Famous equestrian painter George Stubbs (1724–1806) painted Pumpkin with a Stable Lad in oil on a panel in 1774. (© Yale Center for British Art, Paul Mellon Collection, USA)

Muybridge Horse in Motion

The Horse in Motion, a series of photographs taken by Edweard Muybridge, studies the movement of horse "Sallie Gardner," owned by Leland Stanford. The horse ran at a 1:40 gait at the Palo Alto track on June 19, 1878. (Photo used courtesy of the Library of Congress)

Celebrated Trotting Stallion

Artist George Wilkes created this stunning Currier & Ives lithograph of a horse pulling a sulky and driver in 1866. (© Bridgeman Art Library, London/SuperStock)

horse, Abe Edgington, was owned by Leland Stanford, the namesake of Stanford University. Muybridge went on to do many other serial photography projects, many involving horses and some of humans performing different actions.

The Literary Horse

Stories about horses have entertained horse lovers for hundreds of years, providing a sense of adventure and escape, especially to those who don't have horses of their own to ride and care for. Perhaps the most classic tale is *Black Beauty,* written by Anna Sewell in 1887. The story of how the author came to write the book is as intriguing as the tale itself. Due to a bone infection from a badly treated sprain she suffered when she was 14, Sewell was unable to walk. She relied on horses to get around, and she became disturbed by the cruel treatment horses often endured.

As she grew weaker and more bedridden, Sewell decided to write a book to encourage kind treatment of horses. In the story, told from the horse's point of view, Black Beauty is sold from owner to owner with varying levels of care and treatment and he bears witness to abuse of his fellow horses. However, the ending is a happy one and caring horse owners prevail.

After *Black Beauty*, a string of novels about horses followed in the 1930s and 1940s—an apparent heyday for horses in literature. In 1935, Enid Bagnold wrote *National Velvet*. This young adult novel that tells the story of Velvet, a young rider who is determined not only to ride her horse in the famous Grand National steeplechase, but also to win. The movie version of *National Velvet*, which starred a very young Elizabeth Taylor, is perhaps better known than the book.

In 1937, classic novelist John Steinbeck published *The Red Pony*. This collection of stories tells the heart-wrenching tale of a young man who learns the difficult lesson of life and death when his father gives him a red pony.

My Friend Flicka, by Mary O'Hara, followed in 1940. In this equine tale, a strict father and his sensitive son learn a lot about each other by way of a gangly filly named Flicka.

The Black Stallion, published in 1941, is a book with a remarkable history. Written by Walter Farley, an accomplished

horseman himself, while he was still in high school, the original novel went on to be a franchise, totaling twenty books in all. The first book starts with the survivors of a shipwreck—the young Alec and a massive black stallion. While they comb the beaches of their deserted island, they learn to trust one another, and go on to be a remarkable team.

The Nicholas Evans novel, *The Horse Whisperer*, published in 1996, proves that

Black Beauty
Beautiful cover of an 1897 edition of the book.

Showing off Their Paces
An illustration from the 1897 edition of *Black Beauty* portrays a scene from a horse show.

Classics

Marguerite Henry's classic tales of the Chincoteague ponies and their now-famous annual auction are beloved by horse-loving little girls and boys. *Misty* tells the story of how two children set their hearts on owning one of the Chincoteague mares and her foal. *Stormy* follows Misty to her own adult years and the birth of her foal. The same children, Paul and Maureen, and Misty herself also appear in *Sea Star*, the story of an orphan foal and her struggle to survive.

The real reason for my being a jockey...is not to be found in the freedom, the friendships or the travelling that I enjoyed, or even in the great satisfaction of winning races; and it is not in the means it gave me of earning a living either, for if I had been a millionaire I would still have been a jockey. The simple fact is that I like riding horses, and I like the speed and challenge of racing.
–Dick Francis

horse fiction is as popular as ever. The book was the basis for the movie by the same name. *The Horse Whisperer* is in some ways a classic tale of both horse and human overcoming emotional and physical trauma. The plot follows a teenaged girl, who loses her leg and her best friend in a riding accident. Mom packs up the traumatized girl and her equally traumatized horse and takes them far from the East Coast to Montana. There they work with a dashing yet candid horse "whisperer," played by Robert Redford. Incorporating a contemporary trend toward what has come to be called Natural Horsemanship, the horseman cures both horse and girl and has a few doses of goodwill for the mom, too. Pilgrim, the teenager's horse, is portrayed in the movie by a gelding owned by popular horse clinician Buck Brannaman.

One of the most popular writers of horse-related fiction today is octogenarian Dick Francis. Francis, the son of a jockey, was born in Wales. Francis himself enjoyed a successful career as a steeplechase jockey, retiring in 1957 to become a racing correspondent for a London newspaper. In 1962, he published his first novel, *Dead Cert*; it and his subsequent novels, including *High Stakes*, *Blood Sport*, and *10 Lb. Penalty*, center around horseracing. He averaged a novel a year for decades, keeping up his end of a publishing agreement that said if he produced a novel a year, his publisher would keep all his novels in print. Not a huge burden for the publisher, considering most of Francis' novels spend time on the bestseller lists.

Famous Horses and Riders of the Big and Small Screens

As movies became increasingly popular in the 1930s and 1940s, many classic books found their way to the big screen. With the advent of television in the early 1940s, some of these horse tales eventually became hit TV shows, turning their horses and riders into household names.

ROY ROGERS, TRIGGER, AND DALE EVANS

Roy Rogers, the "King of the Cowboys," was born in Cincinnati in 1911 and moved to California at age eighteen. He began his entertainment career singing with The Sons of the Pioneers, with whom he appeared in the Bing Crosby western *Rhythm on the Range*. From there, he went on to make almost one hundred films. And in almost every one of them, his golden palomino, Trigger, was with him.

Rogers (whose real name was Leonard Slye) acquired Trigger (whose real name was Golden Cloud) in 1938. Many legends surround the horse. Some say he died in 1965 at the ripe old age of thirty; others claim that over the years many horses served as Trigger (which is probably true). Rumor has it that when Trigger died, Rogers had his beautiful sidekick stuffed and mounted. A huge rearing replica of Trigger towers over the entrance to the Roy Rogers-Dale Evans Museum and Happy Trails Theater in Branson, Missouri. The horse's prominent placement gives a clue as to who may have been the main attraction during the team's long film and television careers.

Roy and Trigger
Famous cowboy, Roy Rogers, poses for a publicity shot with Trigger, his golden palomino. Known as the King of the Cowboys, Rogers made more than 100 films with his faithful steed.

Roy Rogers and Dale Evans
Roy Rogers, his wife Dale Evans, and of course the beautiful palomino Trigger, were popular film and television stars for several decades in the mid twentieth century. Kids who found this promotional postcard in their mailboxes must have been thrilled.

131

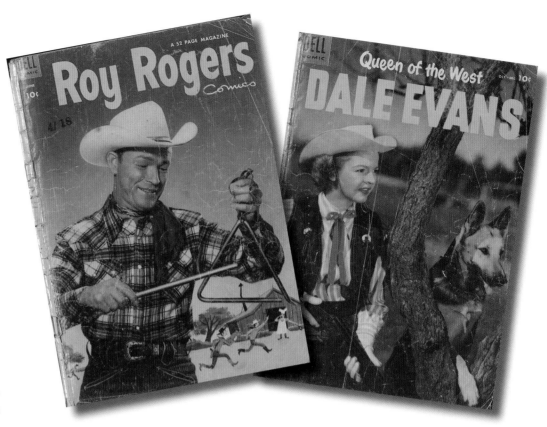

Horses in the Funnies

During the 1950s, young fans followed the adventures of their favorite cowboys and cowgirls through comic books.

Ride 'Em, Cowboy!

Although it may have originated in the American West, this phrase is known around the world. Here's how to say it in different languages:

German: Reiten Sie 'em-Cowboy!

Portuguese: Passeio 'o vaqueiro de em!

French: Montez-les cow-boy!

Italian: Cavalcata 'cowboy di em!

Polish: Pojedźcie 'em kowboj!

Dutch: Kar 'em cowboy!

Phantom of the West Movie Poster

Movies in which the cowboy rode in on his faithful stead to tame the Wild West and save the girl were all the rage in the 1930s, 40s, and 50s. Tom Tyler starred in this 1931 film, advertised as an "All-Talking Serial in 10 Thrilling Chapters."

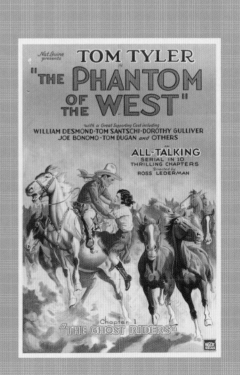

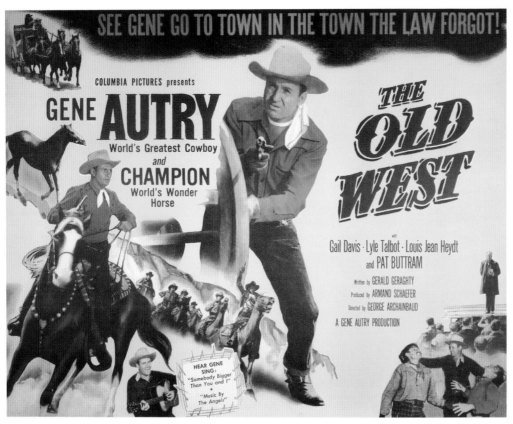

SEE GENE GO TO TOWN IN THE TOWN THE LAW FORGOT!

COLUMBIA PICTURES presents

GENE **AUTRY**
World's Greatest Cowboy
and
CHAMPION
World's Wonder
Horse

THE **OLD WEST**

with
Gail Davis · Lyle Talbot · Louis Jean Heydt
and PAT BUTTRAM

Written by GERALD GERAGHTY
Produced by ARMAND SCHAEFER
Directed by GEORGE ARCHAINBAUD

A GENE AUTRY PRODUCTION

HEAR GENE
SING:
"Somebody Bigger
Than You and I"
•
"Music By
The Angels"

The Old West

As one of America's favorite cowboys, Gene Autry starred in 96 movies between 1934 and 1985. In *The Old West*, filmed in 1952, Gene and his faithful steed, Champion, World's Wonder Horse, clean up the town of Sadderlock. Along with his contemporaries, The Lone Ranger, Roy Rogers, and Dale Evans, Autry brought the horse not only onto the big screen but also into American living rooms via the radio and television. (Image used courtesy of Gene Autry Qualified Interest Trust)

Dale Evans, Roy's singing wife and sidekick in many films and television shows and America's favorite cowgirl, wrote the couple's theme song "Happy Trails" and rode a buckskin horse named Buttermilk.

GENE AUTRY

While we are on the subject of legendary singing cowboys, we can't forget about Gene Autry. Born in Texas in 1907, he moved with his family to Oklahoma, where he worked in the local telegraph office. When Will Rogers went to the station to send a telegram and heard Gene Autry singing and strumming his guitar between busy spells, Rogers encouraged the young man to pursue a career in music. The rest, as they say, is history. Autry, who was known as "Oklahoma's Yodeling Cowboy" early in his career, went on to become famous as a silver screen and musical legend. Gene Autry and his equine sidekick, Champion, played by different horses over the years, starred in many movies together, including *Tumbling Tumbleweeds* (Republic, 1935), *Twilight on the Rio Grande* (Republic, 1947), and *The Old West* (Columbia, 1952). Gene Autry became one of the most popular western stars in the country in the mid-1900s. On the side, Autry owned several

Gene Autry with Champion

Gene Autry was not just a legendary cowboy star of the silver screen, he was also a singing cowboy with a special talent for yodeling. (Image used courtesy of Gene Autry Qualified Interest Trust)

ranches, including the Flying A Ranch in Oklahoma, and he performed in rodeos across the country.

THE LONE RANGER AND SILVER

The so-called "lone" ranger wasn't really so lone. At least equally as well known as the masked man himself was his massive white horse, Silver. With their sidekicks Tonto and his Paint horse, Scout, the Lone Ranger and Silver fought for justice on the big screen beginning in 1938, when Republic Pictures released the first of what would become a fifteen-part serial movie. Audiences were already familiar with the gunman and his horse; "Hi-Yo Silver!" had

Be a Dude

The 1991 movie *City Slickers* certainly did a lot to increase the profile of the dude-ranch-vacation concept. Get out of the asphalt jungle and come live your dream of being a real cowhand, if only for a few days. Go home and impress all your friends at cocktail parties with stories of your cattle-wrangling, bronc-riding prowess. Bore them—I mean, entertain them—with a slide show filled with images of you aboard your own version of Trigger.

High-quality dude ranches offer dozens of other activities besides riding horses. They provide a great way for the horsey set to have a vacation with a nonhorsey person, who might enjoy rafting, hiking, or sitting undisturbed in a beautiful landscape. Many ranches are located in stunning settings adjacent to national parks. You can sightsee and look for wildlife either astride a horse or in a vehicle. Or you can lounge in the lodge hot tub or on a porch swing with a cold drink and a good book, watching the dudes take off or come back from one equine-related adventure or another. Trail rides that culminate in a hearty breakfast at an opening in a field or a steak feed alongside a babbling brook are often part of the offerings.

Anyone Can Ride

Dude ranches and side-of-the-road rent-a-horse stands litter the western part of the country. (Shutterstock Photo)

Mr. Ed and Friends

Okay, Mr. Ed really couldn't talk. In order to get his lips to move, handlers fed the horse peanut butter. Wilbur's long-suffering wife, Carol, put up with a lot of crazy antics during the years the show was on television.

been ringing through living room homes via the radio airwaves since the early 1930s. Matinees were packed Saturday after Saturday. The movies were such a hit that Republic Pictures released another Lone Ranger serial movie in 1939.

The Lone Ranger eventually hit the small screen, and this time two stallions played the part of Silver. Both are reported to have been a Morab—part Morgan, part Arabian. To those who grew up watching the Lone Ranger, hearing the *William Tell* Overture, the theme to the Lone Ranger, brings back fond childhood memories.

FRANCIS, THE TALKING MULE

Francis, the Talking Mule was originally a book of stories written by David Stern III in 1946. From 1950 through 1956, the book was made into seven films. Francis was a U. S. Army mule, and his human sidekick, Peter, was a soldier. Peter was the only person Francis would talk to, which made Peter's life somewhat difficult. When Francis rescued his soldier from behind enemy lines and Peter credited Francis for his bravery, the army thought that Peter had lost his mind and put him away. In a later movie, when Peter becomes a reporter on a big newspaper, Francis helps out again, offering tips he gets from the police horses he befriends. Although Francis's rule is that he talks to no one but Peter, he constantly has to break that rule in order to get his buddy out of jams—with hilarious results.

MR. ED

Francis, the Talking Mule made way for television's *Mr. Ed* in 1961. Mr. Ed wore eyeglasses, followed baseball, and talked, but only to his owner, Wilbur Post, an architect who often had to hide his unusual horse's antics from his long-suffering wife, Carol. A neighbor couple, the Addisons, were regular supporting cast members, but for the most part, it was Ed and Wilbur who kept fans laughing week after week. The show lasted for five years, winning a Golden Globe in 1963 for best TV show, before it ended in September 1966.

The horse that starred as Ed was a beautiful palomino named Bamboo Harvester. His trainer for the television series was Les Hilton, who had also worked on the *Francis, the Talking Mule* movies. Rumor has it that Bamboo Harvester and Hilton were such a great team that scenes were often wrapped in one take. How did Hilton make the horse's mouth move as though talking? By giving him peanut butter, which apparently the horse loved.

SEABISCUIT

The movie *Seabiscuit* wasn't released until 2003, but the great racehorse was already a legend long before that. Brought to life in a wildly successful 2001 book by

Vintage Man-o-War Postcard

Man-o-War was a legendary thoroughbred whose influence on several breeds of horses was immense. He is memorialized with a life-sized statue that greets visitors to the Kentucky Horse Park in Lexington.

"MAN-O-WAR," THE WONDER HORSE, BRED IN OLD KENTUCKY—K15

The Horse at the Grocery Store

Before the automatic doors of the grocery store slid open, you begged your mom or dad or aunt for a dime to ride the child-size mechanical horse that stood in front of the store. If they succumbed, you climbed aboard the cast-iron steed, slipped the quarter into the slot, and got the ride of your life. Remember that? The ride was short in duration, but stayed in your mind at least as long as the boring grocery shopping trip. Plenty of grocery and department stores still have these rides on their sidewalk entrances. You can also buy a coin-operated horse of your own or have one restored at the Carousel Workshop in Florida. Owner Marsha Schloesser has been in the business for over twenty years. She also makes or restores carousel horses.

Ride the Champion

The mighty steed outside the grocery store was the closest some kids would ever get to a real horse ride. But it was worth it! This one is restored and ready to ride again. (Photo courtesy of Carousel Workshop, Deland, Florida)

Lauren Hillenbrand, the thoroughbred Seabiscuit was the darling of the American people. He was said to have given hope to the Depression-era generation. Despite the fact that Seabiscuit was descended from racing great Man-o-War, this horse with crooked legs had a long-shot chance at winning any race. But win he did, putting in an incredible racing career and enthralling a nation with a successful match against his rival, War Admiral. In the movie, Seabiscuit is reported to have been portrayed by ten different horses, from a foal who was the young Seabiscuit (who was supposed to be six months old in the film but was only a month old) to the rearing horse to the Seabiscuit that just stood around.

The Homestretch in Technicolor
The glamour and excitement of the racetrack is a perfect backdrop for the movies.

Jupiter, the Balloon Horse

The circus was the primary source of entertainment during the early twentieth century. This Barnum & Bailey poster, dating from 1904, touts the sensational ascension act of the balloon horse Jupiter, complete with a pyrotechnic display.

Reading and References

Adams, Ramon. *Cowboy Lingo.* Boston, MA: Houghton Mifflin, 2000.

Ainslie, Tom and Bonnie Ledbetter. *The Body Language of Horses.* New York: William Morrow & Company, 1980.

Beckett, Oliver. *Horses and Movement.* London, England: JA Allen, 1988.

Colville, Thomas, and Joanna M. Bassert. *Clinical Anatomy & Physiology for Veterinary Technicians.* St. Louis, MO: Mosby, 2002.

Edwards, Elwyn Hartley. *The New Encyclopedia of the Horse.* New York: Dorling Kindersley, 2000.

Gower, Jeanette. *Horse Color Explained.* North Pomfret, VT: Trafalgar Square, 1999.

Heller, Bill. *After the Finish Line.* Irvine, CA: BowTie Press, 2005.

Hogg, Abigail. *The Horse Behaviour Handbook.* New Abbott, England: David & Charles, 2003.

Howard, Robert West. *The Horse in America.* Chicago: Follett, 1965.

Ipcar, Dahlov. *Horses of Long Ago.* New York: Doubleday, 1965.

Kimball, Cheryl. *The Everything Horse Book.* Avon, MA: Adams Media, 2002.

McCall, Jim. *Influencing Horse Behavior.* Loveland, CO: Alpine Publications, 1988.

Moody, Ralph. *American Horses.* Lincoln: University of Nebraska Press, 1962.

Ohio State University Extension Service Bulletin 762-00, "The Horse's Digestive System."

Slatta, Richard W. *The Cowboy Encyclopedia.* New York: W.W. Norton, 1994.

Vernon, Arthur. *The History and Romance of the Horse.* New York: Halcyon House, 1939.

Waring, George H. *Horse Behavior.* 2nd ed. Norwich, NY: Noyes Publications, 2003.

Index

About the Author

As a child, Cheryl Kimball begged her father for a horse, but the best he would come up with is a plastic horse he found on the beach. She satisfied her horse craving by riding a friend's horse until, at age twenty, she finally bought her own, a three-year-old buckskin Quarter Horse. After two years, she sold the horse and didn't ride or even think much about horses for over a decade. Then the bug bit again, hard. She bought a two-year-old Quarter Horse gelding in 1991 and became so intrigued by learning how to educate a horse that she now has five. Kimball most enjoys working with young horses and writing about her experiences. She has written several books on horses, including *Mindful Horsemanship, Horse Wise, The Horse Show Handbook for Kids, The Everything Horse Book*, and *The Everything Horseback Riding Book*. She writes and rides from the circa-1820s, ninety-acre farm in southern New Hampshire that she and her husband bought in 1993—when she had just two horses.

Photo by Jack Savage